WHAT DO YOU MEAN BY THAT?
The art of speaking and writing clearly

WHAT DO YOU MEAN BY THAT?

The art of speaking and writing clearly

W. G. Ryckman

DOW JONES-IRWIN
Homewood, Illinois 60430

ISBN 0-87094-218-2
Library of Congress Catalog Card No. 80-66024

Printed in the United States of America

1 2 3 4 5 6 7 8 9 0 K 7 6 5 4 3 2 1 0

Preface

This book was written with one very important goal in mind. To improve your confidence in your own ability to communicate effectively.

Time and again, professional people are required to present their ideas to a group or prepare a report to be read by their superiors. The need, therefore, to be clear, concise, and accurate is of the utmost importance. Ideas can easily be confused if the communication link is haphazard.

Unlike many books on the subject of communication, this is not a theoretical book. Rather, the methods presented here come from 40 years of effort to teach myself and others the art of speaking and writing clearly.

It is my earnest hope that what I have to say will be of assistance to you as you strive to achieve your personal objectives.

W. G. Ryckman

Foreword

This is an age in which the walls of space are tumbling down. There are few places in the world which remain unseen and silent. Through the media of television, newspapers, and magazines, we acquire new familiarity with the folkways and byways of lands recollected vaguely from early schoolbook days. Communication is the name of the game as we discuss in authoritative fashion the politics, fashions, and foibles of peoples flashed before us in sight, sound, and print.

A perplexing anomaly exists. While we pride ourselves on our knowledge of the outer countries, it is increasingly obvious that we find it harder and harder to communicate effectively with our next-door neighbors. What we say and think across the fence, in the office, and at home have a way of becoming distorted in the process of translation. Too often we listen but fail to hear. Bill Ryckman recognizes the problem of personal communication and has done something about it. His book is a Baedeker for those who wish to say what they mean and mean what they say.

The Darden Graduate Business School is one of very few institutions requiring a full year of study in analysis and communication. The rationale for this requirement is direct and simple: Business executives are effective only to the extent that they can communicate their ideas in oral and written fashion. In large measure, the lasting value of this exposure to communicative skills is due to Bill's application of business

experience to classroom teaching. This School is greatly indebted to him, as will be the readers of this book.

C. Stewart Sheppard, *Dean*
Colgate Darden Graduate
School of Business Administration
University of Virginia

Contents

1

Breaking the ice

The words *dais* and *rostrum* are roughly synonymous, meaning a raised platform. A podium is a specialized dais used by orchestra conductors; a pulpit is a specialized dais cum lectern used by clergymen. A lectern, strictly speaking, is a reading desk. Most speakers perform standing on a dais behind a lectern. I mention this as it should be of some comfort to them to know where they are when they begin their speeches.

Speakers may also derive comfort from familiarizing themselves with their surroundings before taking their place at the lectern.

Preliminary preparation

Hint:

□ Check the setup beforehand. If you put your notes on the lectern, will you be able to read them comfortably? Is the light adequate? If there is a microphone, is it operating? Don't flick fingers at it yourself; let someone else perform that menial task. If your speech is to be a long one and you suffer from cotton mouth (a dryness induced by nervousness), you should have a glass of water waiting for you secreted inside the lectern. Taking an occasional sip is entirely proper when speaking. Many powerful speakers have been known to sustain their rhetoric by mixing other liquids with the water. Check the access to the dais. If there are steps, count them and be sure there are no obstacles or electric cords in your path. It is embarrassing to fall when making your way to the lectern. Check the distance from where you will be standing to the back of the dais. You will disconcert your audience and perhaps suffer loss of dignity if you step away from the lectern and disappear from sight to the accompaniment of a resounding crash and a shrill scream.

Getting to and away from the lectern

When the bell tolls for you, rise from your seat and move toward the lectern.

Hints:

- Your movements should be unhurried, dignified.
- Do not begin your speech as you mount the steps of the dais. Do not begin as soon as you reach the lectern.
- First, remove your notes from your pocket and place them on the lectern. You have already made sure they are in the proper order.
- Place your watch by your notes so you can be aware of the passage of time.
- Compose yourself; look out at the audience.
- When you have done all this and are quite ready, thank your introducer in not more than a half dozen words and begin your speech.

When your speech is ended, how do you get back to where you came from? It isn't easy.

When your last word has been uttered, you should stand for a short moment, doing nothing. If it is a public affair and there is a smattering of polite applause, you may bow in acknowledgment. If it is a company affair, the big boss casually says, "Thanks, George." In either event you gather your notes deliberately, put them in one pocket, your watch in another and then walk back to your seat, remembering the number of steps you must descend and the location of the extension cords.

Hints:

☐ You do not start your retreat by looking over to the chairman of the meeting with a shy, winsome smile and an expression on your face that translates into, "How'd I do, Dad?"

☐ Don't be in too much of a rush to leave the lectern. Don't go flying off followed by a blizzard of note cards. Take your time and manage a dignified and unhurried departure.

☐ You never start gathering your notes as you begin your final sentence and then sneak away allowing your last words to dwindle to an ineffective whimper in your wake.

☐ Finish your speech before you do anything else.

Body actions and motions

Be very conscious of head and eye movements. Eye contact with the audience is essential.

Hints:

☐ Look at individuals in the audience. Great speakers have the ability to make every member of the audience feel he is being personally addressed.

☐ Do not focus on a single section of listeners to the exclusion of others.

☐ If you have too many notes, you will spend excessive time looking down at them, and your head action will be mainly vertical—like those novelty shop birds that dip their beaks in a glass of water and continue to bob up and down by the hour.

☐ Use lateral head movement as well.

☐ Don't fix your eyes on a spot eleven thousand miles beyond the EXIT sign at the back of the room and keep them glued there except for the glances at your notes.

Hands and arms can be a trial to any speaker. What can be done with them?

Hints:

☐ Let them hang naturally when not otherwise employed. Hands should not be stuck in trouser pockets even if they do not jangle keys or change. Women usually do not have pockets, but they can and often do jangle bracelets.

☐ Do not grip the sides of the lectern with nervous strength sufficient to prevent it from taking off and flying away.

☐ Hands should not be folded against the chest in a gesture of deep religious significance.

☐ They should not be used to straighten clothing, rub noses, explore ears, or smooth down hair.

☐ Arms should not jut straight from the shoulder like ramrods or be placed arrogantly akimbo á la Mussolini.

☐ Gestures should reinforce and complement the spoken word.

☐ Gestures should not be jerkily reminiscent of movements of marionettes.

☐ Gestures should not be similar to the unbraked gyrations of a windmill in a cyclone.

Feet are Fred Astaire's greatest asset. A speaker, however, finds them more of a liability than an asset.

Hints:

☐ Feet should be planted securely on the floor, each leg carrying an equal share of the weight of the body.

- Balance may be shifted occasionally but only for bodily comfort.
- Feet should keep the body at the lectern except when they arc employed to provide locomotion to an exhibit the speaker may be using.
- They should not be used to teeter back and forth.
- They should not perform a soft shoe routine or carry the body on short aimless peregrinations during the speech.
- In general, feet should be neither seen nor heard.

Voice and delivery

No speech can be a success if it is inaudible to the listeners.

Hints:

- Make sure you can be heard by the entire audience. Pick the person furthest from you and pitch your voice to reach him.
- If the auditorium is large and well filled, the microphone should handle the volume problem. If there is no microphone, it is wise to station a friend at the back of the room and he can use simple hand signals to inform you if your voice is coming through clearly.
- On the other hand, don't blast the audience out of its seats by the volume of your delivery. Too much noise frightens listeners, makes them tense and antagonistic.

Speed of speaking

Some speakers are tortoises, others hares, while a third group ebbs and flows like an unsynchronized geyser.

Hints:

- A very slow speaker should not attempt to change himself into a Gatling gun. He can, however, smooth out his delivery by shortening the length of the pauses and developing continuity of word flow.

□ There is one great advantage to a deliberate pace in speaking. The audience is able to absorb everything that is said. Of course, a rapid speaker can say more in a given time than a slow one, but the law of diminishing returns controls when word flow exceeds the listener's comprehension limits.

Rapid speakers have even more problems than slow ones. If a speech is of a complex or technical nature, an unsophisticated audience may fall behind the speaker, miss a phrase or even a sentence, and become hopelessly lost.

Furthermore, if a speaker uses a uniformly rapid pace, he cannot emphasize the vital points he is making. Everything comes out with the same tonal quality.

"Ums," "ahs," and "uhs"

These sounds have identical meanings, and the speaker's individual preference controls his choice of which to use. To many speakers these are the most necessary sounds in the English language. A single one serves as a period to denote the end of a sentence and alerts the audience that a new thought is forthcoming. The same sound uttered twice or more by a moderately paced speaker indicates difficulty in finding the proper word to express the exact meaning of the thought he is attempting to convey. A third use is more esoteric in character. When a speaker's word flow is exceptionally fast, his mouth can outrun his brain. When this happens, there is no automatic noise control shutoff valve on the voice box, and a series of these sounds will erupt until the brain catches up and suggests a new batch of words to be spoken.

How does the speaker control the terrible trio?

Hints:

- □ He records his voice so he can actually hear himself utter the appalling sounds. Until he does this, he will not acknowledge his dependence on them or realize the impression they make on a listener.

- □ He goes over what he wants to say often enough that the proper word will not be difficult to conjure from his mind.

- □ If he is a rapid speaker, he slows his word flow to the point where his mind can keep up with what he is saying. In short, he must learn to listen to himself as he talks and talk only as fast as his comprehension allows him. Listening to yourself isn't as simple as it sounds. Try it.

- □ Recording one's voice and playing back the tape will do more to eliminate the habit than any other remedy.

"You know"

This appears to be two words. It is not; it isn't even one word. It is merely a sound like "uh." Its meaning is somewhat more complex, however. In its early lifetime the expression meant that the speaker had a clear concept of what he wanted to say but was unable to find the words to express himself. Thus, he would broach a subject, mumble a few words about it, and add, "You know what I mean," later shortened to, "You know." This addiction is pure laziness, a slovenly habit that should be attacked ruthlessly. The first time a person with whom you are conversing uses this sound, you should direct at him a fierce stare and deliver a stern admonition, "No, sir, I do not know what you mean. All I know is what I hear you say."

Hint:

- □ Break the habit of "you know." Think before you speak and you will find the use of the sound unnecessary.

Vocabulary

A large vocabulary fluently used is of tremendous value to a speaker. If your choice of words is limited, there are many ways to broaden it, and a number of excellent books have been written that can be of great assistance to you.

Business words or phrases such as *throughput, frame of reference, orchestrate, scenario, point in time* should never be used. Nouns turned into verbs should be avoided like the plague. A law can have an *impact* on a business, but it can never *impact* the business. *Implement* as a verb is gaining in favor, but for an audience to hear it once is sufficient. It is a convenient word to use, but overuse is irritating to a listener. *Hopefully* should never be used under any circumstances. "Hopefully, profits will improve next year." Does the speaker mean he hopes profits will improve? If so, let him say so. *Bottom line* is, at present, much in vogue. It does evoke a clear image of what the speaker means, but again overuse of the words diminishes the effect.

The use of bureaucratic gobbledygook is an insult to the intelligence of an audience. *Action oriented, meaningful dialogue, nonalienated and viable infrastructure,* and similar idioms are collections of letters that look like words but mean little or nothing.

Expressions like these are as offensive to the cultured listener as is a smutty story to the pearly ear of a blushing maiden.

Hint:

☐ Listen to a recording of yourself. How many clichés, junk words, and fad words do you use? Even a few is too many. Expunge them from your vocabulary.

Read or listen to the words of an intellectually bankrupt individual trying to impress an audience with his mastery of technical or business jargon. Do you really want to sound like that?

Profanity

There is no place for coarse words or profanity in a speech made in a serious business environment. You may be sure your audience knows all the words as well as you do, but it is wise to leave them unsaid. A prude might take umbrage at a juicy epithet, and who knows, the prude might be the chairman of the board.

Hint:

□ Keep it clean. Smut and four-letter words are for nightclub comedians. There are no exceptions to this rule.

Technical language

When computer experts are discussing a technical problem concerning their little monsters, they speak in a language incomprehensible to a nonexpert in the field. Yet, they are totally lucid to each other. Similarly, a nuclear scientist using his specialized vocabulary to explain a theory to an uninitiated layman might as well be talking Swahili. In such circumstances, if the purpose of the discussion is to inform, the result will be abysmal failure.

Hint:

□ Know your audience. If you are discussing your thing with equal experts, you may use a specialized vocabulary to your heart's content. But, if you are addressing nonexperts, you should couch your argument in words that will be understood by a reasonably intelligent person without specialized knowledge in the field.

For example, the director of computer services in a mammoth conglomerate, making a presentation to his board asking for a million dollar appropriation for additional equipment, will probably not get his wish if he makes his request in words of which only 10 percent are understood. If, on the other hand, he explains what the new equipment will do in terms that are clearly understood by the board, he has a much better chance of securing his objective.

At times, catering to an audience is an extremely difficult task for a technical expert, many of whom are not experienced speakers. Such an expert should never go to the mat with the board without a trial run.

Hints:

□ He should try his presentation on a friend or a nontechnical co-worker and determine whether he enlightens or confuses.

□ At the same time he shouldn't make the mistake of talking down to an audience in an overzealous attempt to be clear. A majority of board members do understand the principles of simple arithmetic and might resent being instructed how one arrives at a total of four when adding two and two. Only practice and experience will determine the line of demarcation between obfuscation and oversimplification.

Grammar and sentence structure

In general, speeches are not composed of well-rounded sentences. They are inclined to stumble on and on, kept moving by "ands," "buts," "alsos," and the ubiquitous "um" or "ah." Grammar is also a problem. In long rambling sentences it is difficult to keep tenses straight, as well as singulars and plurals.

Hint:

- ☐ Make a conscious effort to speak in reasonably short sentences.

All speakers are guilty of bloopers, mispronounced words, slips of the tongue, and grammatical solecisms.

Hints:

- ☐ You will spot most of these if you are paying attention to what you are saying. Correct yourself calmly and keep going. If you hear yourself say, "He don't," stop, say, "He doesn't," and continue. Do not put a silly grin on your face and say, "I beg your pardon," before correcting yourself.
- ☐ Don't let occasional slips of the tongue bother you. Most will pass unnoticed by the vast majority of your listeners even though they are attentive. If you produce an unconscious but inspired *lapsus linguae,* it is proper to share in the amusement of the audience as did the speaker who inadvertently reversed consonants when intending to refer to the Panama Canal as a busy ditch.

Anecdotes and jokes

The chairman of the board and the president may tell jokes if it pleases them to do so. Their time is not limited as it is for other speakers, and they can rely on a universal chuckle at even the feeblest funny story. What goes for them does not go for you. Stick to your assignment. Keep it strictly business.

Personally, I am offended if a speaker feels he must tell a joke to gain my attention and interest. I am sure some speakers are merely attempting to establish themselves as one of the boys when they act like comedians.

Hint:

□ Leave the jokes and humorous stories to others.

A major digression is necessary at this point to soothe the ruffled feathers of many individuals who enjoy an apropos joke as a prelude to or during the course of a speech. Furthermore, many an excellent speaker has built a reputation on an ability to blend message and wit into a delightful mixture that pleases the most discriminating palate. I have only envy for such a talented person and have no intention of alienating him.

Consequently, I must concede that there may be a place for a well-chosen joke even in a serious talk. Coarseness of expression or offensive subject matter should be avoided, especially if there are a number of strangers in the audience. A wise speaker vets his jokes to assure himself he will not antagonize a single listener.

Do not forget the distinction between wit and smut. Felicity of phrase is one thing, stories about the traveling salesman quite another.

At many convention banquets the principal speaker is chosen not for his preeminence in the profession of the convention members but because of his speaking skills. He may be a successful football coach with a silver tongue and hundreds of amusing stories about national sports heroes. He may be the author of a syndicated column and make a marvelously mirth-provoking speech in which he deflates bureaucratic windbags. Such men are chosen because they represent a welcome escape from the dry technical fare that has been offered all day long by other speakers. The talks such individuals deliver are and should be light and humorous; anecdotes and jokes are essential ingredients.

An argument can also be made, I reluctantly admit, for the use of a joke as an icebreaker at the beginning of a serious talk. A speaker about to launch into a thirty-minute discussion of import quotas and customs duties might find that a well-delivered and pertinent story will make the audience more receptive and even make himself more attractive to it.

I suppose that one objects mostly to an attitude on the part of some speakers that indicates they consider their jokes to be as important as their message and that they have been chosen as speakers as much for the quality of their stories as for their knowledge of the subject.

Good taste should be the arbiter of whether or not a story should be used. Above all, a speaker should beware of those publications that offer a choice of a thousand jokes, half that number of anecdotes about famous people, and pages of quotable quotes, all of which are listed alphabetically by subject matter. Such jokes, anecdotes, and quotes are usually as tired and limp as a chef's salad left for three hours in the hot sun.

Hints:

- □ Remember there is a time and a place for everything, including jokes.
- □ When making a business speech, don't forget that the message is the important factor. The joke is purely supplemental.
- □ There is no place anywhere for coarse vocabulary or plain dirty stories.
- □ Finally, remember that the single person who is offended by a slightly risqué story may be the one person you can't afford to offend.

Personal experiences

You might charge me with prejudice against jokes and anecdotes sprinkled throughout speeches, and I freely admit the allegation. However, I do not object to but enthusiastically endorse the use of personal experiences to enliven and reinforce points made—provided, of course, they fit logically into the speech and do not sound as if they were bludgeoned into place with a sixteen-pound sledge.

"Despite what government spokesmen have said and are saying, there is a shortage of home heating oil. Only last week I . . . ."

"It is illegal to discriminate against women in industry. The law is explicit on this point. Yet, I recently uncovered in my own organization a case where a woman . . . ."

A bald recitation of facts can be arid and sterile; the addition of a personal experience gives animation to the presentation, and it draws each listener into the situation and involves him with what the speaker is saying. Once you involve your listener, you have his attention and it is up to you to hold it.

"People say that scuba diving is perfectly safe so long as basic safety rules are followed. Don't you believe it! One morning last January while diving with Digger Foulkes off Australia's Great Barrier Reef, we were at a depth of eighty-six feet when suddenly . . . ."

Powerful. The speaker can't miss, and as the story unfolds, only the most perceptive members of the audience will realize that the outcome of the harrowing experience cannot have been fatal to the speaker.

How different such an approach is from what is usually heard: "A funny thing happened to me on the way to the Fairmont this evening."

So, use personal experiences to gain and hold the attention of your audience and to support the points you make. Be sure the examples you use actually reinforce your argument. Never force a fit.

"The same phenomenon was observed during the great blizzard of 1888. I remember as if it were yesterday how, on the second day of the storm as I was struggling through drifts as high as my head . . . ."

Notes

Notes are road maps designed to show a speaker where he is and where he is going next. The preparation and use of them is an art that should be mastered. To record notes, index cards three-by-five inches are recommended. There are several reasons for this choice:

1. They fit easily in a pocket.
2. They will not be visible to the audience when placed on the lectern.
3. They are a convenient size to handle when progressing from card to card during the speech.
4. Larger sized cards are more difficult to carry and handle.
5. Sheets of paper are totally unsatisfactory. They don't lie flat on the lectern; they are visible and distracting to the audience. Don't you always estimate the number of pages in a sheaf a speaker draws from his pocket with a flourish as he takes his place at the lectern, and after he has turned to page two, don't you extrapolate the length of his speech? Many times a close estimate of elapsed time is the principal satisfaction derived from such a speech.

Above all, notes should be unobtrusive. The less attention drawn to them the better for all concerned. How many opera goers are aware of the presence or function of the prompter's box?

Preparation of notes
Hints:

□ First of all they should be easily read. There are typewriters with extra large type; if your office has one of these, use it.

If one is not available, use a regular typewriter (CAPS ONLY) provided your eyesight is good; otherwise, print the notes in heavy dark ink. Make it almost impossible to misread the copy. The size of the lettering should be related to the sharpness of your vision. It is decidedly unnerving to glance at a card, see the word PROMOTION, embark on a spirited discussion of the subject, and suddenly realize the word was actually PRODUCTION and that until it and two other issues are disposed of, nothing can be said of Promotion. Speakers have been known to blow their cool in such a situation, and speeches crumble to ashes and dust.

□ Notes should be in outline form and should not be written in sentences. (Exceptions noted later.) If a speaker is well informed in his subject and has planned and rehearsed his speech adequately, he should know what he wants to say in each segment. His notes should serve as a reminder of the sequence of the issues he will discuss and prevent him from skipping one.

Sections of notes that should be written in full

a. The opening sentence of a speech is the attention getter; if it is a good beginning successfully delivered, the speaker at least starts with the interest and goodwill of his audience. A problem exists because the opening of a speech coincides with the period of greatest nervousness of the speaker. Let us suppose that when addressing the top echelon of his organization's sales executives, our newly appointed sales manager intends to start like this: "The new and dramatically improved model of our product is ready for the market at a time when competitive pressures are the heaviest they have been for years." This is heady stuff; our man intends to introduce the new model and lay out a promotion program that will utterly rout the competition. The audience will be eagerly alert, knowing great opportunities and commensurate profits are in store for them as the grapevine has been working overtime ever since they arrived at the home office. Our speaker moistens his dry lips, is conscious of the thudding of his heart and the dampness of his palms. He opens his mouth and this is what comes forth. "The new and improved product of our competitors, uh, uh, is now heavier than ever, you know." Later that same day our hero, being called to the president's office, is told that he will enjoy the climate of Idaho, and the management of the Twin Falls warehouse will be a challenging opportunity.

Hint:

□ Write out the opening of your speech. Make sure you deliver it accurately and emphatically.

    b. The closing section of a speech is equally as important as the opening.

Hint:

□ Write it out also.

    c. It is often difficult to move smoothly from one issue in a speech to another. Continuity and flow are important, so a speaker should prepare his transitions carefully.

Hint:

□ Write out transitions on note cards.

    d. Quotations should be written out in full in the appropriate place on the note card. They should not be copied on separate cards which have an aggravating habit of becoming difficult to find when needed. If an unusually long quotation is to be read from a book, the proper page should be marked by a slip of paper, and the passage to be read should be clearly marked with a colored pencil.

Notes should be made of exact figures that will be mentioned: $1,751,293.17, for instance. Do not attempt to memorize such a number. It is unwise to include a number of figures in a speech without supporting them with an exhibit. The mind can retain only a few figures and, if exposed to too many, will remember none.

For the most part notes, other than the full sentences referred to, should be limited to a word or two per subject. The more terse they are, the shorter will be the glance at them to refresh or confirm the memory of what comes next. The more accomplished the speaker, the fewer are the notes required.

Insufficient notes

Too many notes can cause problems. So can too few. Many speakers overestimate their ability and attempt to waltz through a ten-minute speech without any notes at all. A very few have the virtuosity required to accomplish this tour de force. Too often the ten-minute speech is delivered in six minutes, and when the speaker concludes his presentation, the puzzled expressions on the faces of his listeners are his first awareness that he has neglected to mention three of his most important arguments.

Hint:

☐ Don't try to be too much of a hero. Your manhood will not be questioned if you use a couple of cards to support your memory.

Memorizing a speech

Speeches should never be memorized. A speaker should attempt to impart an image of spontaneity in his delivery.

The audience knows the speech has been carefully prepared and rehearsed, but if delivery reflects all his work, it loses its effectiveness. An actor must memorize his lines, but the secret of good acting is to maintain an air of freshness in a performance. The actor who plays his part mechanically, his body moving woodenly and his voice mouthing his words in a monotone as if reading from a script, will never be more than third rate. Contrast him with the performer who, even in the second year of a successful play, acts and speaks as if the part were being played for the first time.

Unless one is a trained actor, memorized words sound flat, empty, dull, and uninteresting. Little personality comes through, and the words have as much excitement as the canned announcement in Grand Central Station of all the stops on the Norwalk local which will depart in seven minutes.

Unconscious memorization is an insidious malady caused by overrehearsal. Don't practice a speech so assiduously that you fall into the same word pattern each time you go over it. Strive to maintain the semblance of spontaneity; don't always have the next word on the tip of your tongue.

Hint:

□ Rehearse your speech but not to the point that you sound like a recording.

Reading a speech

Speeches may be read:

1. When the material is of such a sensitive nature that even an unconscious change of a word or two can lead to disaster. Examples: when announcing company policy on a new labor contract in a meeting with union officers, or

informing stockholders of a pending price-fixing suit against the company. In both instances every word spoken will have been cleared by the legal department, and nothing may be said other than or beyond what has been approved.

2. When time restraints are so critical that running over even fifteen seconds cannot be tolerated. Normally, such rigorous adherence to a schedule is encountered only when the speech is broadcast on radio or TV.

Under no other circumstances is it proper for a businessman to read a speech. To do so is a callous insult to a listener whose first reaction is that the speaker has asked his assistant to put something together on the subject and that he, too, is hearing it for the first time as he reads it. The effect is heightened if the speaker occasionally stumbles in his reading or comes across a word he can't pronounce. The second reaction is that since it is all written out, why doesn't he distribute copies to everyone and let us get out on the golf course or back to work, depending whether we are at the Homestead or the office. In either event the audience is antagonized, and the speaker's message, even if it is a good one, loses its value.

Academicians read papers at conferences. It is altogether fitting and proper that they do so. A few aboriginal cannibals still make a practice of eating visiting missionaries, and this, too, may be proper according to their lights. A businessman has no more reason to emulate an academician at a conference than to copy a cannibal's habits at the dinner table.

Hint:

□ Don't ever read a speech unless you are forced to by legal requirements or time stricture.

Time limits

It is customary to assign a limit to the length of a speech. Heads of many corporations feel that a limit, once imposed, should be rigidly adhered to, and it ill behooves any underling to exceed his limit by a substantial amount. Few speakers intentionally fail to utilize all their allotted time. Some misguided individuals, given five minutes and believing the assigned subject to be worthy of double that time, deliberately plan a ten-minute speech. A small percentage of them might even be allowed to complete it. Others will be halted unceremoniously.

Hint:

□ Don't try the patience of the big wheels. If they say five minutes, complete your speech in that amount of time and stop. If they want to know more about your subject, they will question you until they are satisfied. Let them be the judges of how much they want to hear.

A problem arises in this connection when a speaker discovers his speech-making word flow is either slower or faster than his rehearsal speed. Five minutes of practice might convert to four- or six-and-a-half minutes delivery time. Experience will teach him what rehearsal time to achieve in order to hit a five-minute performance.

Hints:

□ Find out whether you are a speeder upper or a slower downer. Allow for it.

□ Place a watch with a sweep secondhand on the lectern. Mark checkpoints on your notes to tell you whether you are on schedule or not.

Visual aids

A competent speaker must be skilled in the use of visual aids to clarify and reinforce the spoken word. Appealing to two senses rather than one aids a speaker in getting his message across. Seeing the figure $273,520 makes a more vivid impression on the mind than merely hearing it. A bar or line graph can mean more than a thousand descriptive words. Exhibits of some type are a sine qua non when a presentation relates to technical and quantitative material.

Today's children are introduced to this art at an early age through "Show and Tell" sessions in grammar school. Many full-grown individuals seem not to have progressed much further than their children in the mastery of the art.

Visual aids come in various shapes and forms, and an executive should be familiar with the use of most of them if he is to be considered a competent speaker.

The most commonly used media for exhibits are:

1. Easel flip charts.
2. Viewgraph.
3. Slides.
4. Films.
5. Samples.
6. Blackboard.

At the end of this section you will find examples of good and bad exhibits.

1. Easel flip charts

Because this device is simple, it is widely used. It has a number of advantages. Perhaps the most important of these is the fact that it is not necessary to turn lights off and on continuously. Effective use can be made of color. If a speech is to be made away from your office, it is not necessary to transport bulky or fragile equipment. All you need is a roll of exhibit sheets, as an easel is usually readily available wherever you are. However, don't take chances on availability. Check beforehand. A speaker has little difficulty in positioning himself by his charts so he can face the audience while he uses a pointer or a pencil to direct attention to the fact or figure he is discussing.

Unfortunately, there are a few drawbacks to the use of easel flip charts. If the audience is large, it is difficult to make words and figures of sufficient size to be seen by everyone. Also, some rooms are so designed that people sitting up front at the sides cannot easily see a centrally placed easel. In addition, because of their relatively small size, easel charts must be simple and cannot contain a great deal of information.

Nevertheless, flip charts are an easy and effective means of presenting visual information to an audience, provided the physical environment is favorable.

Now for some specifics on the preparation and use of flip charts.

Hints:

□ Always leave a blank sheet between two charts. The purpose of this is twofold. If colored marking pencils are used to draw the charts, the lines of the next chart will show through. Also, if the speaker desires to say a few words after completing the use of one chart and before moving to the next one, he can turn to the blank sheet and not distract the eyes of the audience with old business or beat the gun on new business.

□ Make sure the lettering is large enough to be seen clearly from the distant reaches of the room. The only way to determine this is to test legibility. Level of lighting will affect results, so will glare and shadows. Don't ask a gimlet eyed youth to stand at the back of the room and accept his approval of the size of the lettering. For all you know, the president might be a back row sitter, and you don't want to strain his myopic, ancient eyes.

☐ Keep it simple. Don't put a hundred figures on a sheet or have sixteen lines running every which way across the chart. Don't try to cover too much on a single exhibit.

☐ Use color for purposes of differentiation. Color is attractive and eye catching. Should you stick to complementary colors and avoid clashing mauves and puces? Don't ask me. Use your own judgment.

☐ Have an artist prepare your exhibits. This is important. The best exhibit will fail if the lettering or figures are sloppily drawn. Unless you are a competent draftsman yourself, get someone who is to make your charts for you. Pleasing appearance is a decided plus. Whether you do the work yourself or have it done for you, check word for word and figure by figure that spelling is accurate and numbers correct.

☐ Double check and triple check to be sure the sheets are in the proper order.

☐ Make sure the clamp fixing the sheets to the easel is secure. Nothing can be as distressing as flipping over one sheet and having the whole mess slip from the stand and cascade to the floor. What does one do if this should occur? There is no satisfactory answer, so don't let it happen.

Let us assume our charts have been drawn by a fledgling da Vinci, they have been securely fastened to the stand, and have been pronounced readable from the back row by an elderly gentleman with half inch thick lenses in his glasses. We are now about to use them (the charts, not the glasses). We introduce the subject of the first exhibit and walk confidently to the easel.

Hints:

- ☐ Turn back the blank sheet to reveal the first exhibit.
- ☐ Stand to one side of the easel so that as you face the audience, you can see the exhibit out of the corner of your eye.
- ☐ Address your remarks to the audience. It is permitted to glance at the exhibit, but it is not permitted to talk to it.
- ☐ Use a pencil or a pointer to direct the attention of the audience to the specific part of the exhibit you are discussing.
- ☐ Under no circumstances should you read what is written on the chart. The words and figures are large enough to be seen by everyone, and it would be impolite to give the impression you doubt if the audience has learned to read.
- ☐ Use the material on the chart to reinforce or substantiate what you are saying.
- ☐ As you will be away from the lectern and your notes while working at the easel, it might be helpful to put light pencil notations in the margin of the charts to remind you of what you want to cover on that particular sheet. The notes will be visible only to you, and you must resist any impulse to lean down and peer intently at an unintelligible scrawl you have made.
- ☐ The last notation will remind you of the content of the next chart so you will be able to make a graceful and timely transition to it. Have the foresight to dog-ear or fold up the bottom corner nearest you of all the sheets on the easel. This will enable you to turn to the next chart without fumbling with the sheets or even upsetting the easel in an attempt to separate two pages stuck perversely together.

Some speakers prefer to use stout cardboard sheets instead of pads of flip chart paper. Exhibits prepared thusly do look more impressive, but several problems may be encountered when they are used. Transportation is difficult. Flip chart pads can be rolled while stiff charts cannot be folded, and it is often inconvenient to carry a number of three-foot square sheets of heavy cardboard. Furthermore, what do you do with a chart when you have finished using it? It must be removed from the stand and put out of sight somewhere. If it is placed behind the others on the stand, there is a danger that all may slip to the floor.

In any event, manipulation of cardboard charts is much more difficult than merely turning over a sheet of heavy paper. Individual charts do, on occasion, get their proper order confused. Sheets attached to a pad cannot.

All things considered, flip charts are the easiest and most foolproof visual aids that a speaker can utilize. I recommend that an inexperienced person employ them in every situation where they can be used effectively. Having mastered the art of flip chart management, he may then venture on to the other media.

2. Viewgraph

Much more information can be put on a viewgraph transparency than on a flip chart. Most viewgraph exhibits can be typed, thus eliminating the necessity of finding an artist. In addition, it is no problem to make a transparency of printed material. This allows easy preparation of exhibits. Legibility should not be a problem as long as the screen is of sufficient size and the machine the correct distance from it.

These advantages are substantial, but viewgraph use does present serious problems. Lighting can be an aggravation since lights must be turned down when the viewgraph is in use and turned up when it has served its purpose. This requires the services of a switcher on and offer. Another assistant may be required to place the transparencies in position on the machine. A system of signals must be developed if the performance is to run smoothly. Remember—the more people involved, the greater the opportunity for mix-ups.

Hints:

- If an assistant is working the machine, the speaker will stand to one side of the screen and must have a pointer long enough to indicate the figure or fact on the exhibit he is talking about.

- If the speaker operates the machine himself, a pen or pencil can be used to indicate the proper spot on the transparency and the pointer will show on the screen.

- He must be careful not to obtrude his head, hands, or other parts of the body on the screen. This is irritating to the audience and restricts view of the exhibit.

- The machine will probably be close to some of the audience, and the speaker must be sure not to obstruct anyone's view.

- Regardless of who operates the machine, the transparencies must be kept in proper order.

- Gremlins have been known to turn transparencies upside down and even reverse them.

- Beware of too many figures on a viewgraph exhibit. Don't reproduce a whole page of a phone directory if you are interested in two numbers only. Include in your exhibit only what needs to be shown. Failure to observe this precept is the most prevalent error in the use of the viewgraph.

- Schedule your viewgraph exhibits so they flow continuously from beginning to end. The purpose is to restrict lighting changes as much as possible. Don't scatter your exhibits throughout your speech at two-minute intervals. At the same time, remember that an extended period of semidarkness might cause a goodly portion of your audience to succumb to the blandishments of Morpheus.

3. Slides

Slides make a most effective impression as they have the great advantage of being in color. Like the viewgraph they depend on mechanical equipment and the manipulation of light switches and thus are subject to the vagaries that afflict the usage of all such equipment. A further complication is added if the projector is not automatic and requires the services of an assistant. If a control unit at the end of its long umbilical cord makes the assistant unnecessary, one problem is exchanged for another. Not all remote control equipment always works as competently as the advertising would suggest.

It takes a master of the art to handle slides smoothly. Otherwise, the act is reminiscent of a Marx Brothers extravaganza. Slides and related equipment are expensive. If cost is a factor, other methods of displaying exhibits should be considered.

Hints:

□ Don't be too extravagant. A few slides go a long way. Flashing one picture after another on a screen in such rapid succession that the viewer gets only a blurred impression will defeat the purpose of the display. Give the audience time to see what it is looking at. Too many pictures in too short a period is the major error of the inexperienced slide user.

□ When a new slide is flashed on the screen, stop speaking for a few seconds to allow the audience time to study the picture.

□ The room will be darker than it would be if the viewgraph were being used. Be sure you can read your notes in the gloom.

□ Rehearse with your assistants. Make positively sure your slides are in the proper order and right side up. Test your equipment beforehand.

4. Film

To be used by true professionals only. Consider what happens if the entire speech depends on the movie and something goes irretrievably wrong with the equipment or the film. Always prepare for the worst.

Film is even more expensive than slides. Bulky equipment must be transported and set up. Easel exhibits are the simplest, film the most complex. Yet, high-grade color film is dramatic, impressive.

Hints:

□ The film should be produced by a professional. Homemade amateurish work will detract from rather than add to a presentation.

□ Test everything that can be tested. Was the film rewound after the previous use?

5. Samples

It would be an all-time first if a product manager of a new breakfast food did not display a sample of the new package when introducing it to a group of company executives. He might even have samples for every member of the audience, and he would distribute them *after* the conclusion of the presentation.

A shipbuilder might be excused if he did not bring his new half-million-ton oil tanker to the meeting room, but it would be surprising if he did not have a miniature model on display along with beautiful pictures of the real thing.

People do like to see what the speaker is talking about, and it makes sense to give them an opportunity to do so. Showing samples would seem to be a simple matter, but there are rules to the game that should be observed.

Hints:

□ If only one product is being presented, the sample may be left in view throughout the presentation after it has been introduced. If more than one are on the agenda, get the cereal box out of sight before you unveil the new toothpaste tube. Don't allow competition with what you are showing at the moment.

□ Don't have samples visible until you introduce them. It is easy to conceal one small item in a pocket or behind the lectern. If you have a number of different samples, keep them out of sight in a box, and after each has served its purpose, put it into another box.

□ Never distribute samples to the audience while you are speaking. No one will listen as he inspects, reads, tastes, or even drinks the sample. No distractions!

□ When dealing with a number of items, make sure you extract them from their hiding place in the proper order. It is not considered professional behavior to talk dramatically of your revolutionary and radically innovative ball peen hammer and then flourish a chrome-plated socket wrench before the startled eyes of the audience. Get your act straight.

□ If an article is too large to be concealed by normal means, throw a cloth over it and when the time comes, do like Prince Charles who, when dedicating a statue, is reported to have said that although he had little experience with statues, he had, in his time, unveiled a few busts.

6. Blackboards

Finally, a few words are appropriate on the use of this medium for exhibits. For generations, blackboards were indigenous to schoolrooms, and the distinguishing feature of a teacher was chalk dust on his or her clothing. Times have changed, and many meeting rooms now contain a few square yards of blackboard.

There appears to be a basic urge lurking in every human breast to seize a piece of chalk and demonstrate one's knowledge and authority by covering a board with cabalistic runes and hieroglyphics one fondly believes are written words. Usually the audience can neither decipher what you write nor hear what you say while you are writing. Stay away from the blackboard.

SAMPLE EXHIBIT I

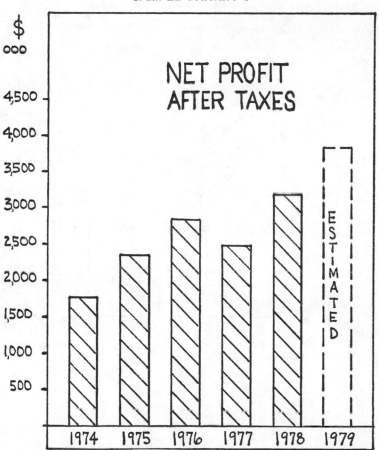

A good exhibit. Uncluttered, clear and easy to understand.

SAMPLE EXHIBIT II

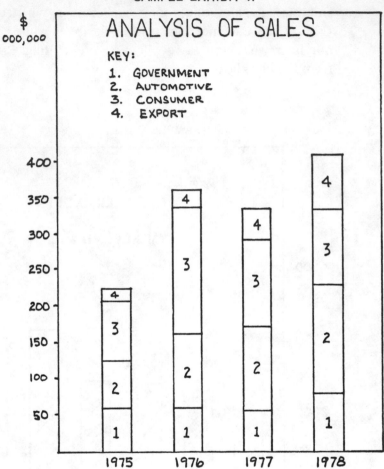

Good. Simple. No problem to understand. Bars not junked up with writing. Keyed numbers do the job.

SAMPLE EXHIBIT III

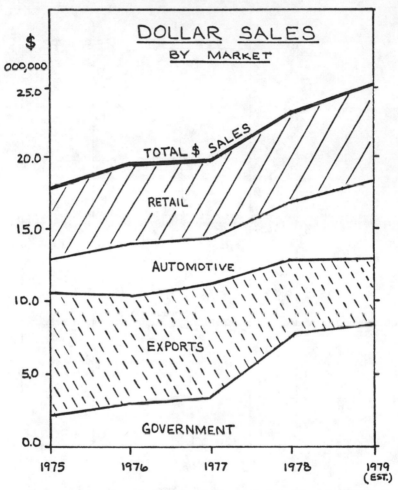

Another way to show information similar to that contained in Exhibit II. Easy for the reader to follow and understand.

SAMPLE EXHIBIT IV

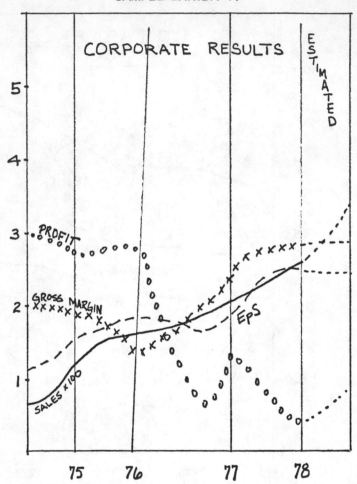

Terrible. An insult to a viewer. Reminiscent of the spoor of four morose moose meandering across the frozen tundra after a snowstorm. Clutter. Impossible to interpret scale on vertical axis for the four elements on the graph. What is EPS in 1977; 2, but 2 what? Also, it appears unlikely that earnings per share (EPS) could increase at a time when profit is declining. Difficult to follow the progress of the lines. Only good thing is that lines are differentiated. The perpetrator of this monstrosity should join his moose in Manitoba.

SAMPLE EXHIBIT V

PRODUCT ANALYSIS

BY REGION

I EAST

Drugs	42%
Food	11
Cosm	28
Soft D.	8
Beer	4
HARD	5
MISC	2

II MID-SOU

Drugs	27
Cosm	14
Sof D	30
Beer	11
HARD	1
Misc	15

III SOUTH

Drugs	40
Cosm	10
Soft D	8
Beer	4
HARD	10
Peanuts	8
Tobacco	26
MISC	?

IV MIDWEST

Drugs	27
Cosm	10
Soft	12
Beer	8
Hard	10
MISC	30

V S·West

DRUGS	50%
Food	23
Cosm	11
SOFT D	6
HARD	8
misc	11

VI GULF

D	61
F	11
C	8
S.D.	9
Hard	12
Beer	0

VII N-WEST

D	41
F	10
C	9
S.D.	8
H	12
B	10

VIII Far West

D	42
F	8
C	11
S.D	12
H	12
B	14
Misc	3

Horrible. Too much on one exhibit. Difficult if not impossible to compare regions. Why not bar graphs as in earlier examples? Careless lettering. Columns do not always add to 100 percent.

Slovenly. Person who prepared this exhibit got bored and sloppy. Fire him!

Being oneself

Perhaps the most valuable lesson a speaker can learn is the absolute necessity of being natural. He cannot force himself into a mold he does not fit. What is good for one person will not work for another. Some speakers are charmers and can talk the birds out of the trees; others exude sincerity and are believed as soon as they open their mouths; while still others are effective because it is immediately apparent they are masters of their profession.

Each speaker should operate from his strength, build on it, and base his delivery on it. At the same time he should attempt to shore up his weaknesses so that he becomes a well-rounded, effective speaker.

Hint:

□ Be yourself. Improve whatever areas you are able to, but under no circumstances ever try to be what you are not.

Conquering nervousness

No human has ever or will ever totally conquer nervous tension when approaching the lectern to make a speech. Hardened professionals suffer the same queasy qualms that afflict the veriest tyro. Those who profess to be free of such fears are either mythomaniacs or so devoid of emotion they can scarcely be considered members of the class homo sapiens.

The difference between the expert and the rookie is that experience teaches a person how to control his nerves and how to present an outward-appearing serene and confident demeanor to the audience. To the public his composure is immaculate; inwardly his seething vitals are twisted into coils of copper wire that inhibit breathing and even cause his heart to palpitate. Yet, he bows graciously to the man who has introduced him, says, "Thank you, Mr. Folett-Smith," looks out at his audience with a benign smile, and begins his speech.

Confidence is the key. Once this euphoric state is achieved, the heart resumes its beat, the mind begins to function, and a speaker feels at home in his environment. The sources of confidence are many and varied. Linus has his security blanket; when it is clutched tightly in his hands, he can face the world's tribulations with equanimity. Without it he is reduced to a terrified rabbit.

A speaker's security blanket is a patchwork quilt with many pieces of material contributing to his feeling of confidence. First, there is a comfort in knowing he is properly groomed for the task at hand.

Hints:

☐ The first duty of a speaker is to check appearance and dress. All of you are probably familiar with the story of the man who moved from a rural area of Iowa to Greenwich, Connecticut. Every morning of a working day he observed his neighbors performing a never changing ritual as they stood for a moment on the front porch before entering their cars to drive to the station. For many weeks he was impressed by this seeming act of devotion before facing the rigors of the daily battle for survival in the jungles of Manhattan, and it was not until much later that he realized the deed had a more practical application: wallet, commutation ticket, did I forget my necktie, are my trousers zipped? If the speaker substitutes notes for ticket, he will do well to emulate those Greenwich tycoons.

☐ Shirts and suits should be immaculately pressed, shoes should glisten like mirrors, hair, which is no longer merely cut, should be effectively styled and in place.

While waiting, a speaker should study the surroundings.

Hint:

- □ He should examine the room with an analytical eye, noting the doors, the decorations, the height of the ceiling—everything that will help make it familiar while looking out from behind the lectern. He should scrutinize the audience, try to break it down to individuals rather than an indistinct mass of strange faces. The more familiar he is with the surroundings, the more comfortable he will feel.

Many speakers attempt to begin a speech in a breathless state. This does not inspire self-confidence.

Hint:

- □ While being introduced, the speaker should take a number of deep breaths. This might steady breathing and heartbeat, and it will charge the lungs with life-giving oxygen.

Meticulous preparation is a wonderful confidence builder.

Hints:

- □ If the speaker has prepared and rehearsed the speech adequately, he can draw comfort from that fact. If he has not, he has only himself to blame for the ensuing disaster.
- □ If his notes are well written, he should be assured that even if he suffers a lapse of memory, a glance at them will put him back on the track.
- □ The opening sentence of his speech is written out at the top of his first note card. Delivering it firmly and accurately will give him confidence as he continues.

Confidence builds on itself. Nervousness abates when the speaker realizes he is off to a good start.

Hint:

□ The early sentences of a speech should have been practiced over and over again.

Once the speech is well launched, the speaker will begin to feel, to be aware of the surroundings, even to think. The mind will gradually take control of the vocal process, and delivery will start to flow evenly. The body, however, operates on a different time schedule and may lag behind the mind in conquering its feeling of strangeness and unease. It can perform in an odd and erratic fashion unless it, too, is rigidly controlled.

Practice is the only means of ridding the system of its natural tendency to act in singularly peculiar ways. Practice in private will not help to any great extent. There is little nervous tension involved when one addresses an empty room and none when rehearsing in the comfortable privacy of one's own boudoir. So, actually speaking before an audience is the only answer. Prepare as well as you possibly can and then let nature take its course.

A speaker with no experience can, and usually does, deliver a five-minute speech without being aware of anything except a feeling of abject terror for the whole period. The next time he speaks, his palms will not be quite as damp, and the fog will last only four minutes. If he survives his early experiences, by the fifth speech he will know where he is and what he is doing when he reaches the lectern. Being in this delightful frame of mind, he will be able to perform more than adequately since he will have conscious control over his voice, his speech patterns, and the motions of his body.

He will still, of course, be nervous, but he will have learned how to control the evidence of his nervousness and thus win the envy and respect of his audience.

Self-improvement suggestions

Aspiring authors should write; aspiring speakers should speak. That is excellent advice for gaining proficiency in both arts, but speaking, not being a private accomplishment, offers fewer opportunities for self-expression. Yet, there are a number of positive steps an individual can take in order to improve his speaking ability. The first requirement of a budding speaker is to gain confidence and ease while speaking. As these increase, the outward signs of nervousness will decrease.

Hint:

□ He should actively seek speaking opportunities. There are many in the community, and these are excellent practice. They have a special advantage since mistakes made away from the office while he is developing self-confidence and proficiency will not have a negative influence on his business career. Appearances at Rotary and Lions Club meetings, church functions, school affairs, and inclusion on programs of professional and social organizations all help.

At the same time there is much an individual can do to improve his speaking without the presence of an audience.

Hints:

□ First of all he can read aloud. This is a wonderful experience for learning to use the voice to complement the spoken word. The musical direction, *con simpatico*, with feeling, is what he should strive for. Another Italian phrase *con brio*, meaning with animation, is also worth remembering. A printed word has a specific meaning. The same word can be spoken in a dozen different ways: varied emphasis, inflection, degree of loudness or softness, and so on, so that it takes on a dozen different shadings of meaning. Our speaker will not become an actor like Olivier, but he can learn the rudiments of the art. So, let him talk to himself, read to his children. *The Three Bears* has tremendous dramatic possibilities. If he has no children, let him address his dog. Dogs are wonderfully attentive, and despite an occasional tendency to fall asleep like human audiences, they are most friendly listeners.

□ Poetry makes the best material for practice reading. Verse has rhythm and cadence; it is good to develop these speech patterns when improving one's own style. The voice is important when giving poetry its full meaning.

□ Get away from the monotone, the unvaried sentence structure; vary delivery speed, use pauses for emphasis. Learn to add excitement to your voice. Read this type of material:

"Friends, Romans, countrymen . . ."
"This is the forest primeval . . ."
"Fourscore and seven years ago . . ."
"When in the course of human events . . ."
"T'was brillig and the slithy toves . . ."

□ Have fun while you are reading.

□ Learn to read without gluing your eyes to the printed page. Practice until a glance will record the line in your memory. This is excellent training for proper use of notes when making a speech.

I once had a friend who developed a unique and highly successful cocktail party act. He would read a list of names and addresses from a phone directory, and in his reading he covered every emotion known to man: excitement, ecstasy, despair, triumph, pathos—you name it, he had it. For an encore he would read a dozen or so phone numbers. It is truly amazing what the human voice can do. Develop and train yours.

Hints:

☐ When you talk aloud to yourself, use a recording device and play back your performance not once but several times. When you listen, be alert for:

1. Quality and timbre of voice.
2. Smoothness of word flow.
3. "Uhs," "ahs," "ums"; count them. If you are afflicted with the bug, the number will astonish you. You will note a few even if you are reading and are forced to look down at your material before you thought you would have to.
4. How about sentence structure? Do you connect clauses by an "and" or an "also" and continue ad infinitum? Count the number of times you do this.

The other night I watched and listened to a television interview with a woman whose husband occupies one of the most important positions in our country. She appeared perfectly at ease: calm, self-possessed, her voice clear and pleasing to the ear. Yet she seldom uttered a simple sentence. Most were a page in length, kept limping along by an unending stream of "ands" with the only punctuation supplied by an even greater number of "uhs." What she said made a good deal of sense; the pity of it was that her message was destroyed by her delivery. The interviewer, by contrast, exemplified all the virtues of an accomplished professional. The experience reinforced my conviction that spouses and close family of high public officials should be seen and not heard.

After that slight digression let us get back to our numbers.

5. If you are a fast speaker, time the Gettysburg Address at your natural pace. Try it again. Can you slow your delivery?
6. If you speak too slowly, try speeding up.

7. Keep records of elapsed time on a recitation repeated at intervals over an extended period of time. Has delivery pace improved?

8. Is your tone flat, do you fail to emphasize important words or phrases? Listen for the development of drama and excitement in your voice. Are you conquering the monotone?

9. How about your vocabulary? Tell your friendly tape recorder what you did that day, what corporate victories you won, what you told the taxi driver who tried to run you down as you dashed across Vanderbilt Avenue. Grade yourself on the quality of the words you used, except, of course, those directed at the cabby.

10. How is your grammar? Listen for slips of the tongue. What about the use of slang, coarse words?

11. If your company has videotape equipment, set it up in an empty room and talk into it so you can both see and hear yourself.

12. Head and arm movement. How do your hands act when not in use? What about notes? Is your head continually bowed to them? Do you speak with a smile or an expression of abject terror on your countenance?

Hint:

□ Practice, practice, practice.

2

Speeches

By now you have served your apprenticeship during which you have been exposed to many of the do's and don't's of speechmaking. You have assimilated scores of helpful hints and learned to recognize the pitfalls that await the unwary speaker. It is high time for us to leave the schoolroom and move into the real world where speeches are not discussed objectively but actually prepared and delivered.

In a moment or two we will meet a banker, the first of the bevy of speakers who will be our mentors in the pages that follow. As usual, however, I will make a few general remarks about speeches before turning the baton over to him.

Nearly all speeches fall into one of two basic categories: expository or persuasive. Some contain both elements. There is a fundamental difference between the two types that cannot be ignored.

When making an expository speech, one must "tell it like it is" without embellishment and be totally honest and impartial in presenting the issues involved. The point of the speech is to convey all of the available information and allow each member of the audience to draw conclusions from his personal analysis of the material presented. The secret to making an expository speech is to accumulate relevant material and to present it clearly in a well-defined order. The speaker must recognize that there are at least two sides to every question and that each should be fully explained without any attempt to sway the listener in one direction or the other.

In a persuasive speech the speaker also ferrets out and reveals to the audience all information germane to the situa-. tion. While the expository speaker stops when he has done this, the persuader goes on to present and support his personal conclusions in an attempt to convince the audience to see the matter as he does.

Personal integrity is very much at issue here. The ethical persuader must be honest in his presentation of the facts. The con artist shows only one side of the coin: for example, he focuses on the potential 1,000 percent profit and ignores the 100-to-1 probability that the profit will not be made and the enterprise will go bankrupt. He may tell the truth but certainly not the whole truth, and it is unlikely that his statements will be nothing but the truth. The executive who prostitutes his principles to sell his plan is a fool. Management that is played for a sucker neither forgets nor forgives.

As a consequence, the executive will find it advantageous to stick to the straight and narrow, not only when making an expository speech but even when persuading the boss to go along with his recommendations.

Preparing an expository speech

Let us assume you are a banker and the annual conference for the banks in your region is being held at the Grand Hotel, Point Clear, two weeks from now. Your tennis game has been unusually sharp this spring due mainly to the success of your efforts to develop a Borgian top spin forehand, and you confidently expect to be a shoo-in for the doubles championship. Your chances have not been diminished because you had the foresight three years ago to hire for your department the number one singles player on the University of Florida team, and you have been able to include him for the first time in your bank's delegation to the conference. His youth and raw power are excellent complements to your deft finesse and mastery of court tactics.

For the first time in several years you have not been given a speaking assignment at the conference, and it was a considerable surprise when the president of the association called this morning and informed you that a half hour was being reserved for you on the Friday morning program. It appeared that a new set of regulations covering an area of your supposed expertise is being proposed by the Federal Reserve Bank, and if the regulations are issued in the form that present rumor suggests, they will have a serious effect on the banking community. Your assignment, the president explains, is to discover what the Fed actually proposes, research the issues involved, and make a report to the bankers attending the conference.

Your first move is to arrange a trip to the Fed in Atlanta where you hope to get the straight story on its plans. Your next action is to put your tennis partner to work studying the present regulations on the subject. Both of you will then get on the phone with other banks to find their first reaction to the proposed regulations. At the same time you will be discussing the matter with other executives in your own bank.

By the end of the week your research is complete. You have found that the proposed regulations are not precisely what it was first feared they would be. You have also learned the Fed's timetable in issuing them and the lead time before they will become effective.

You are now ready to organize your speech. For this purpose you make use of an outline. It looks like this:

I. Statement of situation
II. Proposed regulations
    A.   Timetable for effective date
III. Present regulations
IV. Changes under new policy
 V. Possible effects on banks
    A.   Good and bad
VI. Courses of action open to banks
    A.   Accept the regs as proposed
    B.   Object across the board
    C.   Ask for revisions
VII. Summary and conclusions

Sections I through IV are straight reporting and cautious analysis. This is where the mettle of your young tennis partner is tested. You check his work carefully, for you know that if he misread or misinterpreted a word or a paragraph of bureaucratic gobbledygook, it is you who must take the blame if the banking community is given inaccurate information. When you are convinced you are on solid ground, you fill in the outline with the points you will cover in your speech.

Section V is where the action is. This is what the audience will be most interested in. It is here that your own experience will stand you in good stead. In this section you will draw heavily on conversations with officers in your own bank and with bankers throughout the region.

You must be totally objective in your presentation for this is purely an expository speech. Personal prejudices and preferences must be curbed, as you are doing a reporting job only. There is a distinct difference between a news reporter and a news commentator. You must observe the distinction.

Section VI is straightforward. Again, you merely state the alternatives and give no indication of your personal feelings in the matter.

The final section should be short. You will give a brief summary of the possible effects of the new regulations and remind the audience that if the association or individual banks wish to take action, they have so many days or weeks to do so.

You make no suggestion as to what stand the conference should take. That will be up to the chairman of the meeting. He may open a general discussion to see if there is a concensus of the members present. It is possible that a committee will be appointed to learn the attitudes of the banks in the region and to prepare for discussions with the Fed on the proposed regulations. Assuming you have made a successful speech, it is more than likely you will be named chairman of the committee. Lots of luck!

The foregoing should take care of the mechanics of preparing the contents of the speech. Much still remains to be done.

First of all, let us consider the audience you will be addressing. It will be composed entirely of bankers, many of whom will be known to you, which is a great advantage. In such an environment, your manner will be more relaxed and less formal than it would be were you addressing total strangers. On top of that your research and study will have made you more knowledgeable on the topic than anyone in the group you are addressing. Knowing your subject and knowing your audience are the two most important factors in reducing the nervous tension when you begin your speech.

Your notes will be rather more complete than usual, as accuracy is essential when dealing with government matters. You will prepare a marked copy of the proposed regulations so it will be easy for you to read sections of them.

Your opening and closing statements will be written out exactly as you will deliver them. Transitions should be no real problem, as the speech outline flows naturally from one segment to another.

Rehearsal, however, will still be important. You will have a lot to cover in half an hour. A trial run of your speech will be necessary to determine delivery time. If you are overlong, you must condense or eliminate; if you are a few minutes short, you will not pad your speech. The balance of your time can be devoted to answering questions posed by the audience.

Being an old pro and expecting to have about seven minutes for questions, you guard against total silence when you call for questions at the conclusion of your speech. You write out a couple you can ask yourself and another to ask the audience. This should be enough to get the ball rolling. Based on previous experience you will not prime a friend to ask the first question. (More than once the stooge has been either dozing or left the room at the critical moment.)

On Thursday you spend three and a half hours in the large meeting room listening to other speakers. As you listen you are busy casing the joint. Are the acoustics good, does the microphone always work properly, is the lectern of a reasonable height, did anyone trip while ascending or descending the dais? In general, is the audience attentive, is there a constant flow of people entering and leaving the room, what is the average noise level?

Small matters, it might seem, but the more a speaker knows of his environment and his audience, the fewer surprises lurk in the underbrush and the more relaxed he will be when beginning the speech.

In the evening you extract $9 from a Mississippian who, despite compelling evidence to the contrary, foolishly considers himself a superior backgammon player, and then retire to your room. But not to turn in quite yet. You pull your speech notes from your suitcase and lay them out on the bureau. You kick off your shoes, plug in your trusty tape recorder, push the button and say, "Good morning. I have been asked to explain . . . ." No good. You rewind the tape, retrieve your son's stopwatch from your shaving kit, wind it, push the starting button, push the recorder switch, and start again. This time all systems are go; twenty-three minutes and fourteen seconds later you stop the recorder.

Now is the time to get out of your clothes and into your pajamas. You felt comfortable talking; your notes gave you just the amount of assistance you needed, and for the first time, you were able to read sections of the proposed regulations without stumbling over the awkward phraseology.

As you play back your speech, you make careful notes. Only four "ums" in twenty-three minutes—not bad. They all came within a ten-second span during which you lost your train of thought when switching from reading a regulation to explaining its import. Two more run-throughs of the section clear up the problem.

The most difficult part of the self-appraisal, you have found, is to listen only to what you say and pay no attention to all the additional information in your mind. The audience will hear only your words, and they have to be the right ones if they are to carry the intended message. Your listeners will not be mind readers.

Two spots in your speech need rewording for clarification. You get them straight and rewrite your notes so you will not go astray again tomorrow.

The close comes through somewhat tentative, and you rewrite your final two sentences on a new note card. The beefed up version is much better, so you rehearse it several times and then record the final three minutes of your speech. On playback it comes through clear as crystal and with just the right tone of voice.

Now for bed. You sleep soundly, secure in the knowledge you are primed and ready for your speech. The semifinals of the tournament are scheduled for the afternoon, and at breakfast your youthful partner assures you he retired alone to his room at an early hour the previous evening and was in a reasonably sober condition. All is well.

We have spent a goodly amount of time with our banker friend over the past two weeks and have invaded his privacy for a couple of hours on the evening before his speech. We have gotten to know him rather well, and it may strike us as curious that we do not know his name. Yet, this does not prevent us from learning from him.

Has he been too conscientious in the preparation of his speech? Has he spent more time on it than it deserves? After all, at a conference who really devotes full attention to what is being said? Our banker rarely, if ever, thinks of such matters. His own standards require him to do his best no matter what the circumstances. Who knows when or from whom the offer of the presidency of an important bank will come to him. The smart executive keeps all his lines open, and one ear is constantly cocked, awaiting opportunity's first knock.

Our banker is an experienced and competent speaker. His competence is based to a large extent on a comprehensive method of preparation. No one in any profession reaches the top without training and stays there without practicing and employing his skills.

Many years ago I had the opportunity to observe an application of these characteristics in action. I had invited a top sales executive of my company to attend a banquet in my territory. Fred arrived Friday afternoon; we had dinner, exchanged gripes and company gossip for a couple of hours, and retired early. Saturday would be a busy day with a full schedule culminating in the banquet at our hotel in the evening.

At midnight the night manager awakened me and in an agitated voice asked if my friend was quite normal. No true salesman ever is, but when the manager told me my guest was behaving oddly in the banquet room, I rose, dressed, and went downstairs where I met the manager. We tiptoed to the banquet hall which was in almost total darkness. Bare round tables surrounded by chairs covered the floor; a lectern sat at the center of a wooden trestle that would be the head table the next evening. Barely perceived in the deep gloom, standing behind the lectern was Fred rehearsing his speech in tones loud enough to reach every nook and cranny of the hall.

Unobserved by Fred I led the manager softly away. "Close the doors quietly," I told him. "Return to your copy of *The Saturday Evening Post*. My friend is harmless."

Fred had addressed hundreds of meetings similar to the one he would attend the next night. He was a master of his art, yet he left nothing to chance, and for his last rehearsal he chose the spot where he would deliver his speech.

I returned to my room, rooted around until I found my sketchy notes, placed them on the bathroom sink, and talked to my image in the mirror until I was satisfied with my own banquet speech. This all happened long before the era of the portable tape recorder.

3

Presentations

The purpose of a presentation is either to instruct, to convince, or to do both. The types of presentations a businessman can be called on to make are myriad. It might be a solo performance to the board of directors of his company, a group effort to equally ranked executives, a consultant's recommendation on a promising acquisition, an advertising agency's pitch to gain a new account, a banker's appearance before the State Banking Commission to protest a proposed ruling. All these situations are different, but the varied presentations will have many points in common.

Visual aids are used extensively in presentations, and competence in their development and use is essential to a successful performance. The polished presenter is master of the use of the easel, the viewgraph, slides and movies. There is an art to visual presentation, and competence does not come without experience and study.

It is not unusual for a report to be written on the same subject on which a presentation is made. When this occurs, three different situations can arise, and each will have an important effect on the content of the presentation. Let us examine them.

Presentation made some time after submission of report

Many corporations supply members of the board of directors an agenda of an upcoming meeting and a packet of material relating to the matters to be discussed. For example, the production, marketing, and financial vice presidents might submit a report on operations in their areas for each meeting. These reports would be studied by the board, and at the meeting the representative of each functional area would be asked to make a presentation supplementing the report.

It would be a serious mistake for these officers to waste the time of the board by reading the report. Directors, on an average, are men who regard their responsibilities seriously, and it would be an insult to assume they had not studied the material made available to them. It would even be a blunder to make a short synopsis of the report.

What material, then, should be discussed in the presentation?

Hints:

□ The alert executive has his lines of communication well greased up and down the corporate ladder. He should be alert for and sensitive to reactions on matters discussed in his report. If anything was unclear, he has the opportunity to clarify it. Perhaps a short discussion of background material will add strength to the report or it could be that a more complete analysis of why alternative solutions of a problem were not recommended will further support his conclusions. These issues would be covered in his presentation.

□ The presentation gives the officer an opportunity to mend any fences that were sagging and also gives him a means of updating the report if anything has transpired in the interval since it was submitted. In addition, he might want to answer questions before they are asked and in general put himself at the disposal of the board should it wish to discuss any facet of the situation.

In short, the officer's unstated but implied position is this: "You have read my report; here is additional material you might want to consider. These are new factors that have recently arisen, and I am here to answer any questions you might have." All of this adds up to an excellent opportunity for the executive to enhance his reputation and status.

Report distributed at the time the presentation is made

In many organizations this is standard operating procedure, but an executive must watch his step very carefully if this is the way his company works. He is surrounded by mine fields and tank traps, hooded cobras lurk in the underbrush, and piranhas snap at his ankles as he wades through puddles.

Let us suppose copies of his report are passed around the table as he rises and begins the presentation. What happens? No one pays the slightest attention to what he is saying for the first five minutes. Each individual in the audience is noisily riffling through the report to see how long it is, to find whether his own department is mentioned either favorably or unfavorably and perhaps even trying to read the first and last pages in the hope of getting an advance clue to the speaker's conclusions or recommendations.

Hint:

□ Never, never pass out any written material at the beginning of a presentation. Circulate the report after the conclusion of the presentation.

If the presenter adroitly finesses this pitfall, he is immediately faced by another. He knows he must not read his report, but at some time his listeners must know what he is talking about. This causes a complete reversal of roles between the report and the presentation. In our first example, when the report was distributed prior to the presentation, the report was the important vehicle in communicating information, and the presentation was supportive of the report. The reverse is true here, and the presentation becomes the lead actor.

Thus, all the nuggets of wisdom are crammed into the presentation, the analysis must be concise and lucid, and the conclusions, recommendations, and course of action must be spelled out in detail. The presentation must stand on its own feet, complete and self-contained. The report marshals the supporting evidence to give credence to the presentation and validate its premises.

The presentation is the thing; the report provides the foundation and support for every conclusion made in the presentation.

Hint:

□ It is essential that an executive understand the role reversal between report and presentation in the two situations referred to. In neither case should there be the slightest confusion as to what material should be allocated to each method of communication.

Presentation made first, followed by a report at a later date

This is the best of all possible worlds. Reports have a nasty habit of coming back to bite the writer. The written word endures forever in dozens of personal and public files, and years later an error in judgment, written in black and white for everyone to read, can return to haunt the unsuspecting author. A report that is not written until after a properly conducted presentation is given can avoid a large majority of the slings and arrows that can contuse the author who must write his report without the benefit of a prior presentation.

The advantage is illusory unless the executive who makes the presentation is perceptive and sensitive. Agility in footwork is also an advantage. Here again, throughout the presentation, the argument, as in the second example, must be complete, lucid, and encyclopedic in coverage down through conclusions and recommendations. The difference, however, is great. In this instance the presentation is not the last word; it is merely the probing reconnaissance that is a prelude to the main event, which is the report, and the report need not be written for at least a week.

As he talks, the skilled presenter is alert to any reaction he observes in the eyes or the actions of each of his listeners. His perceptive antennae are operating at maximum efficiency. He notes what appears to be generally acceptable, what causes frowns of disagreement. He is sensitive to the failure of his listeners to understand a complex technical argument. If he unwittingly invades the bailiwick of the vice chairman's pet project, he senses he is treading on slippery ground. Basically he sees where his argument is strong and discovers where it is weak.

Now, our executive is not a con artist; he is an intelligent, ethical man who is convinced his solution to the problem is the best course of action for his company to take. At the same time he is enough of a pragmatist to realize that no small part of his function is to make his solution palatable to his superiors if he would gain their approval for his recommendations. Along with his other talents, he must be a salesman.

So, he stores away in his memory each frown, each smile, each indication of interest or boredom he has observed. If, at the end of his presentation, he has an opportunity to answer questions thrown at him, he must be adept at fielding them. He must be prepared to retreat from too hard a stand on one point or strengthen too weak an attitude on another.

When his presentation is concluded, he should have an

excellent understanding of what his report should contain when he writes it. Weak points will be shored up; some conclusions will be tempered as the result of a better understanding of high-level policy concepts of which he had previously been unaware.

When he writes his report, the enduring document should reflect his best thinking refined by his perception of the attitudes, likes, and dislikes of his superiors. His conclusions will still be his own, but they will be expressed in terms that he feels will give them the best chance of acceptance by the senior management of his company.

Hints:

☐ Every job is a selling job. Never forget that.
☐ Perception and sensitivity are essential characteristics of a successful executive.
☐ Do whatever can be done to make it easy for your bosses to go along with what, in your best judgment, is the proper course of action for your company to take.

Hints on group presentations

It is customary to assign a group to make a presentation when problems or issues are wide in scope and cut across departmental lines. To be effective, a presentation by a group should be a cohesive argument blended smoothly together and not a number of individual speeches delivered in sequence. All too often, however, it turns out to be the latter because the group's organization and planning have been faulty.

Consultants frequently use the group format when making a final presentation to a client, and corporations, too, have learned the value of this method of approaching problems covering several associated functional areas in the organization.

Unsuspected problems arise when a group is involved, and awareness of these will contribute to the success of the group effort.

1. Picking a leader

It is essential that the group has a head who should conduct meetings at which the content and method of the presentation is discussed and responsibilities are assigned to each member. If it is difficult for the group to choose a head because of departmental rivalries or personal jealousies, the presentation will suffer. Consulting firms normally do not encounter this problem as it is customary for one man to be picked to be in charge of the job, and he chooses his group dependent on the nature of the assignment.

A corporation may or may not act in this way. If top management picks the leader of the group and assigns others to it from the various departments involved, all will be well provided the right man has been chosen as leader and his mandate is clear.

If, on the other hand, management merely picks a group of men from various areas and gives them a joint assignment, difficulty may ensue. The group might accept its senior member as leader, an especially forceful individual might assume leadership, or the group might attempt to function as a committee to make all decisions. Any of these solutions can create problems.

Hint:

□ Wherever possible, encourage top management to designate the person who will lead the group and give him clear authority over the assignment.

2. Number of speakers

A short presentation does not lend itself to contributions by all group members. Too much time is spent moving from one speaker to another, and the performance is jerky, unnatural, and unnecessarily complex. A fifteen-minute presentation can be handled easily by one man provided he is familiar with all the material. It would appear unnecessary to include a person in a group presentation if his contribution would be only two or three minutes in length. A six- to ten-minute segment would perhaps make his contribution desirable.

Hint:

☐ In allocating time and choosing speakers for a group presentation, the controlling factor must be the benefit to the presentation rather than concern for the egos of the members of the group.

3. *Allocation of responsibilities*

Let us assume that production, marketing, and financial areas are involved and that two representatives have been appointed to the group from each of these departments. The legal aspect of the situation is extremely sensitive, and an officer of the legal department has been designated as leader of the group. Let us also assume that a maximum of forty minutes will be allocated for the presentation that will be made to the top executives of the company. There is to be no written report.

At a meeting of the seven principals, the matter is discussed, and assignments are given to the representatives of the three functional areas. Further meetings will continue the discussion, and a consensus will eventually be reached. Note that normally there is no place for a minority report on a corporate assignment of this type. The individuals are expected to work out their differences and develop a plan acceptable to all.

At this point the leader must decide what form the presentation will take. He must select the speakers, allocate time to each, and decide on the individual who will open the presentation as well as who will handle the final summary and recommendations.

Hint:

□ In choosing speakers the leader must be ruthless. The most skilled speakers must be used even though they are not senior members of the group or even of their own departmental representatives.

The leader may decide that three speakers should make the body of the presentation and that he will handle the opening and close.

Hints:

□ The leader should realize that while some men do not enjoy speaking and therefore would be relieved not to be selected as speakers, others, and quite often the weakest performers, will feel affronted if they are not chosen.

□ Each speaker should be given a time limit that must be observed.

□ In his opening remarks the leader should give a short rundown of who the speakers will be and the subjects they will cover.

□ If the speakers are known personally to the listeners, a certain informality of introduction is permitted. If they are not, a speaker should not fail to introduce and identify the next speaker at the end of his part of the presentation.

□ Transitions from one speaker to another must be handled smoothly so that there are no abrupt leaps from one area of consideration to another. In short, each speaker must give the next man a strong lead-in.

- ☐ Members of the group who do not speak should assist with the visual aids. Rehearsal is necessary so that they are handled smoothly and unobtrusively.

- ☐ It should be the responsibility of the leader to ensure that the presentation is a cohesive whole, not several segments that do not blend together.

- ☐ He must make sure that one speaker does not repeat information already given by another and also that all necessary issues are covered.

- ☐ The entire presentation should be carefully rehearsed. Nonspeakers in the group will be the best judges of the adequacy of the presentation. They should also be prepared to comment on the speaking mannerisms of the individuals who will make the presentation.

- ☐ It is not easy to criticize a peer. Tact and sensitivity are called for, but if something is lacking in the performance of an individual, he must be apprised of the weakness.

- ☐ A great deal depends on the capacity of the leader to mold the group into a smoothly operating unit. His own effectiveness in opening and closing the presentation will have an important effect on its success.

- ☐ A presentation is no stronger than its weakest link. There can be no glory for an individual if the whole presentation is not a success. Excusing an inferior speaker by saying he meant well cannot justify his dynamiting an important presentation.

Preparing a persuasive presentation

Receiving advice on how to handle a situation is entirely different from actually handling it. How did you feel as an aspiring parachutist, after hours of meticulous preparation and training, when you were pushed for the first time from the open door of the plane?

Let us, therefore, enjoy the experience of watching the preparation of a presentation.

Dave Lloyd, sales manager of Peter Hope, Inc., has been asked to recommend a course of action for his company, a West Virginia food wholesaler that sells to restaurants of all types and to a much lesser extent to schools, hospitals, and similar institutions.

The stated corporate goal is profitable growth. At present, sales are approximately $10 million a year, having doubled in the past five years. Gross margin on sales is 18 percent. Profits after taxes are in the range of 5 percent of gross sales, high for the industry, and the company's financial position is excellent. Present facilities are adequate to handle a 40 percent increase in sales.

Selling is done through twelve salesmen who work the territory and one who handles large chains such as McDonalds, Burger King, and so on. Compensation is paid at rates averaging 3 percent of sales. The house account salesman is paid a combination salary and commission. Salesmen pay their own expenses.

At present there are five selling territories: the areas around Charleston, Beckley, Logan, Huntington, and Welch/Bluefield. The company believes, probably correctly, that if any more men were added to the territories, morale would suffer and several excellent men might be lost. The company also believes that it cannot realistically expect much increase in sales from its present sales force. Salesmen's earnings average in excess of $20,000 a year, excellent pay for men who were formerly route salesmen for bread companies, clerks in supermarkets or assistant managers in fast-food outlets. Experience has taught the company that once a man of this background earns a little more than he needs to get along and is better off than a majority of his friends, the urge to do still better is lacking.

It is clear that, if the company is to continue to grow, new territories must be opened. For valid reasons the owners wish to stay within the boundaries of West Virginia, where there are really only three areas in which expansion is possible: Parkersburg, Wheeling, and Morgantown/Fairmont/ Clarksburg. Population in the rest of the state is so scattered, and restaurants so far between, it would be unprofitable to service these rural areas.

There is one other possibility for increasing sales in present territories. In Beckley, Logan, and Huntington the salesmen sell to only a handful of institutional accounts—schools, hospitals, and so on. The men in question are not comfortable in this type of selling, and since they find it difficult to cover their regular restaurant customers, there is no reason to believe they would resent the addition of salesmen who would develop and handle only institutions on which the regular salesman had never called.

Deliveries are made by company trucks two or three times a week. The expense of operating a truck, including all costs, is slightly less than $100 a day.

The board of directors to which Lloyd will make his presentation is composed of Hope, a man in his late thirties, his mother, who is a substantial stockholder although inactive in company operations, the vice president and general manager, the treasurer, and three outside directors: a banker, a lawyer, and the president of a coal company with headquarters in Charleston.

Naturally, Lloyd knows a great deal about the company that has not been mentioned here. Yet, we have enough information to follow his analysis and conclusions on the expansion problem. It can be stated that he has no argument with the appraisal of the situation as presented.

Lloyd is under no delusion as to his position. He has been asked to make recommendations that will lead to increased sales and greater profits for the company. His solution must be realistic and well supported, yet, no matter how right his conclusions are, the board will not go along with him unless his presentation is clear and convincing.

With this in mind he marshals his knowledge of company operations and the opportunities and alternatives that are available. Once the material is gathered, he prepares a skeleton outline of the presentation he will make. It works out like this:

     I. Present situation.
    II. Necessity for growth.
   III. Possibilities for growth.
       A. New territory.
       B. Add institutional man or men.
   IV. Preferred alternatives.
    V. Costs.
   VI. Expected results.
  VII. Recommendations.
 VIII. Course of action.
   IX. Wrap-up.

You will note the orderly sequence of the outline. It proceeds logically from step to step, and each section leads smoothly into the one that follows.

Dave's next job is to flesh out the outline. In doing so he will list the points he will make in his presentation. We won't go through the whole outline with him, but this is what he has to say on the first section.

  I. Present situation.
     A. Sales doubled in last five years.
     B. Profits satisfactory.
     C. Company in excellent shape.
     D. Capacity adequate to support growth of 40 percent.

  E. Resources available if further expansion of facilities is required.

  F. Summary—all systems go for expansion.

As he continues working, the solution of the expansion problem becomes apparent to Dave. He will recommend adding three salesmen, one each in Morgantown, Fairmont, and Clarksburg. He will also recommend putting an institutional man in Huntington and another in the Beckley/Logan area. Figuring the costs and probable returns of this program requires analysis, but Dave was never afraid of figures and works out his projections, making them on the conservative side and supporting his assumptions as fully as possible.

Once Dave has his presentation fully planned, he has several important items remaining on his agenda.

1. Developing his opening and closing statements.
2. Spelling out clearly his recommendations.
3. Preparing the exhibits.
4. Making the notes he will use during his presentation.
5. Rehearsing.

Opening and closing statements

Lloyd works with three of the directors on a daily basis. He considers all of them to be friends, but, even so, he wants to set the proper tone for his presentation in his first sentences. Dave has been around long enough to realize there is a fine but clearly established line between members of the board and even the most highly regarded executives who are not board members.

He considers starting his presentation thusly, "I am about to present to you a plan that will make a contribution of nearly $100,000 to the company in its first year and almost $300,000 in its second year."

Such a statement is certainly dramatic, but it sounds like

grandstanding to Lloyd, and he knows the board well enough to realize it doesn't go for white rabbits pulled from hats. He discards this opening and starts again.

"Peter Hope has been a successful company in the past. Its sales have doubled in the last five years, and profit margins continue to be excellent. If the pattern of profitable growth is to be continued, the company must find a way to expand its selling territories and at the same time increase sales from present territories without disturbing the morale of the sales force."

He likes that. The statement contains a stroke to management for doing a great job with the company, and the mention of expansion plus the implication that more can be done in existing areas without threat to morale will pique the curiosity of every board member. It is three sentences, not one, and the last is rather involved, but he feels the statement will set the exact tone on which he should build his presentation. So, for the moment, at least, he settles on this opening.

Now for the close. Lloyd wants to end the presentation on a positive note. He is convinced that his plan is the best possible one for the company to take. He is enthusiastic about it and wants his enthusiasm to show through loud and clear. Yet, he is not selling on personal charisma or an emotional display of forensic bombast. A majority of the board is realistically pragmatic and will be convinced only if his plan and his presentation are solidly based on facts and reasonable projections.

How does this sound? "In the development of the plan I am proposing to you, I have considered and analyzed every fact that appears germane to the situation; where projections or assumptions have been made, I have tested each to assure it is sound and realistic. It is my best judgment that the recommended course of action will enable our company to continue its pattern of profitable growth."

This sounds dignified, sincere, and, Dave hopes, convincing as well. For the moment he accepts the statement subject to revision if a better thought occurs to him later.

Recommendations

The most vital part of this presentation is the statement of the recommendations; Dave knows he must have them spelled out clearly and exactly. This is what he writes:

"Since the projections, although in my opinion conservative and realistic, appear so favorable, *I recommend* that we add one salesman in each of the cities of Morgantown, Fairmont, and Clarksburg and two institutional salesmen, one in Huntington and one in the Beckley/Logan area. *I also recommend* that the following actions be taken to put the plan into effect."

The statement is restrained but strong, and it makes a perfect lead-in to the course of action that will follow.

Visual aids

Dave had commissioned a professional technical draftsman to prepare the map (Exhibit I) which would be projected by the viewgraph on the blank wall at the end of the boardroom. The financial charts would be shown on an easel and Dave made them himself. He knows he has his numbers right, and he has put a lot of time and effort into preparing the exhibits but for some reason they are constantly on his mind. He can't decide why this should be, but he has lived with himself long enough to know he shouldn't ignore his intuitive reactions.

Finally, he attaches the pad containing the exhibits to an easel which he carries to the boardroom and places on the spot it will occupy when he makes the presentation.

The boardroom is rectangular in shape with a long table placed centrally in it. Lloyd has been called to board meetings often enough to know that the members habitually occupy the same seats meeting after meeting. Mrs. Hope always sits at the head of the table. To her right is Arthur Robins, the coal man. Next to him sits John Hilker, the lawyer, and to his right is the treasurer, Tom Kelley. To Mrs. Hope's left is Len Smith, the banker. Joe Weldon, the vice president, is next in line and Archie Hope sits at his left. Dave will make his presentation at the far end of the table, about six feet from the nearest board members, Hope and Kelley.

Lloyd turns back the cover sheet of the pad, revealing Exhibit II. He walks to Mrs. Hope's chair and looks at the exhibit. Not too bad. Mrs. Hope is no spring chicken, but she should be able to see it clearly. Pacing off the distance to the easel he finds it to be a bit over twenty feet. He turns to Exhibit VI and gingerly sits in Mrs. Hope's chair, looking around to make sure the door is closed before he does so.

Terrible. He knows what is on the exhibit, and he has little trouble reading the figures, but would Mrs. Hope be able to? Not a chance. He suddenly recalls that Len Smith must be well into his seventies, and when he comes to meetings, he is always driven by one of the young men at the bank. He wears thick glasses.

The exhibit is too cluttered. So much is written on it that the words and figures have to be so small they can't be easily read. That goes for Exhibits IV and V also. The three of them will have to be revised; material will have to be eliminated or additional exhibits prepared. How can he have been so stupid?

The worst mistake he could make would be to ask the whole board to move closer to the easel. One doesn't push people around when he is a guest in their home. Nor could he move the easel to the side of the table. That would mean three people would have to turn their chairs around.

Another thing. He is a salesman not an artist, and the exhibits look amateurish. What the hell was he going to do? He carries the easel back to his office and glares at Exhibit VI. Damn, damn, damn.

Dave providentially recalls that Linda Dennis, the purchasing agent, had once been employed as a commercial artist. He arranges to borrow her services for a day, explains what must be done and gives her the exhibits.

The redrawn charts are ready the next afternoon, and Dave is delighted with them. Linda had placed an asterisk (*) next to every estimated figure so the board would know it was an assumption, not a fact. During his presentation, every time Dave comes to an asterisk, he will explain the basis of the assumption.

He makes a light pencil notation, visible only to himself, on the margin of each exhibit to remind him what the next one covers so that when he finishes discussing Exhibit II, for example, he will glance at the note "institutional men" and say, "We have discussed costs and break-even requirements of the three new salesmen. Now, what about the same information on the institutional men?" He will flip the sheet, and there it will be.

He also folds up a corner of each sheet so there will be no fumbling when he turns to the next exhibit.

Notes

Dave Lloyd is an old pro when it comes to running a sales meeting or making a presentation. A word or two means as much to him as a whole paragraph would to a less experienced man. He has the further advantage that he knows everything there is to be known about the selling operations of Peter Hope. As a result, his notes will be unelaborate and terse. They are memory joggers rather than suppliers of information he is unfamiliar with.

His first note is, of course, his opening statement written out exactly as he intends to deliver it. Subsequent notes follow along with his presentation, and he will probably make little use of them until he reaches his prepared spiel on recommendations. From then until his close he will freewheel most of the way with an occasional glance at his cards to be sure he is leaving out nothing.

A long time ago Dave got into the habit of putting hand-written suggestions and instructions to himself on his typed note cards. These can be seen on the cards reproduced at the end of this chapter.

Rehearsal

The night before the board meeting Dave stalls around in the office until everyone else has gone home. When he is alone, Dave sets up his equipment in the boardroom, closes the door, and goes to work.

The map looks great, the exhibits are beautifully clear, and his spiel is smooth as silk. He runs through his presentation twice, decides to beef up support for his projections of second-year sales for the new men, and when he finally switches off the lights, he is satisfied he has done everything he can to make his presentation a success.

The presentation

Finally, the appointed hour arrives. Dave faces the board confidently. He knows his plan is good; he does not doubt his ability to present it effectively. His exhibits are well made and models of clarity. When he is done, Archie Hope poses a couple of questions which he answers without hesitation. Dave is then excused from the meeting but is called back ten minutes later and instructed to proceed exactly as he had recommended.

It must have been a good presentation. Why was it successful; what virtues did it possess? Let us analyze them.

1. The presentation was strictly business. It was well-organized, delivered in a professional manner.
2. It was clear, well explained. Questions were answered before they were asked.
3. Coverage was complete. All angles were explored. Alternatives were considered.
4. The figures were all there, and they added up right. Exhibits were legible and easy to follow.
5. Assumptions and projections were made, but each was supported to the point that a reasonable person would conclude they were valid or attainable.
6. There was no attempt made to snow the listeners with rhetoric.
7. The course of action was spelled out in specific terms. There was none of "you should do something about this, and see that the other thing is accomplished." The plan was laid out in detail; who does what and even timing was covered.
8. The report was specific enough that the board could say, and did say, "Lloyd, do exactly what you propose."
9. Above all, the presentation and plan were logical, reasonable, and convincing. Lloyd made it easy for the directors to go along with him.

Great job, Dave. Our congratulations!

EXHIBIT I
Map of West Virginia showing sales territories

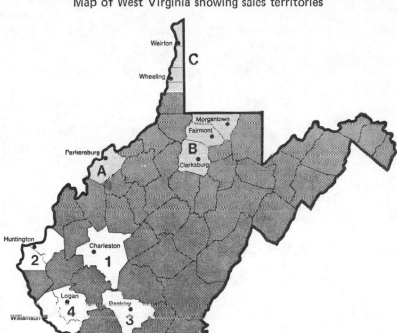

Existing Sales Territories

1 Kanawha County, Charleston City
2 Cabell & northern Wayne Counties, Huntington City
3 Raleigh County, Beckley City
4 Logan & Mingo Counties, Logan & Williamson Cities
5 McDowell & southern Mercer Counties, Welch & Bluefield Cities

Potential Sales Territories

A Wood County, Parkersburg City
B Monongalia, Marion, & Harrison Counties, Morgantown, Fairmont, & Clarksburg Cities
C Wheeling - Weirton area

EXHIBIT II

Ⅱ

COSTS — 3 SALESMEN — 1ST YEAR

SALARY	3 × $10,000	$30,000
TO OPEN TERRITORY		12,000
FIXED COSTS	$3,500/MAN	10,500
* DELIVERY		9,750
	TOTAL FIXED COSTS	$62,250

SALES NEEDED TO BREAK EVEN

COMPANY GROSS MARGIN	18%
COSTS TO COVER	$62,250
SALES REQUIRED	$350,000

EXHIBIT III

III

COSTS — 2 INSTITUTIONAL MEN — 1ST YEAR

SALARY   2 × $10,000 $20,000

FIXED COSTS $3500/MAN   7,000

TOTAL FIXED COSTS $ 27,000

SALES NEEDED TO BREAK EVEN

COMPANY GROSS MARGIN   18%

COSTS TO COVER $27,000

SALES REQUIRED $150,000

EXHIBIT IV

IV

DO FIGURES IN II & III APPEAR REASONABLE ?

AT PRESENT 12 MEN SELL $8,500,000
  FOR AN AVERAGE OF . . . . . $ 710,000

3 NEW MEN NEED SALES OF $ 350,000
  FOR AN AVERAGE OF . . . . . $ 117,000

ONLY ABOUT 1/6 PRESENT AVERAGE

---

2 INSTITUTIONAL MEN NEED
  SALES OF $ 150,000
  FOR AN AVERAGE OF $ 75,000

PRESENT IN-HOUSE MAN SELLS $1,500,000

EXHIBIT V

SALES EXPECTED AND CONTRI-BUTION — YEAR 1

V

THREE NEW SALESMEN

PRESENT MEN AVERAGE	$710,000
* NEW MEN ESTIMATE	24%
EXPECTED SALES PER NEW MAN	170,000
THREE MEN	510,000
GROSS MARGIN @ 18%	$ 91,800
TOTAL FIXED COSTS (EX II)	62,250
CONTRIBUTION YEAR 1	$ 29,550

TWO NEW INSTITUTIONAL MEN

* EACH MAN EXPECTED TO SELL	$250,000
TWO MEN	500,000
GROSS MARGIN @ 18%	$ 90,000
TOTAL FIXED COSTS (EX III)	27,000
CONTRIBUTION YEAR 1	$ 63,000

EXHIBIT VI

PROJECTED RESULTS — YEAR 2 — VI

* NEW SALESMEN EXPECTED TO SELL
MINIMUM OF 50% OF CO. AVERAGE

3 MEN × 50% × $710,000 = $1,065,000

MARGIN @ 18% $ 191,700

* SALARY & EXP. $ 50,000
* DELIVERY EXP.   13,000
                    63,000

CONTRIBUTION $ 128,700

* INSTITUTIONAL MEN EXPECTED TO
DOUBLE SALES IN YEAR 2

$500,000 PER MAN × 2 = $1,000,000

MARGIN @ 18%   180,000

COMMISSION @ 3% $ 30,000
ADD'L FIXED COSTS   7,000
                    37,000

CONTRIBUTION $ 143,000

Dave Lloyd's notes for presentation

READ THIS DAVE + READ IT RIGHT (1)

PETER HOPE HAS BEEN A SUCCESSFUL COMPANY IN
THE PAST. ITS SALES HAVE DOUBLED IN THE LAST
FIVE YEARS AND PROFIT MARGINS CONTINUE TO BE
EXCELLENT. IF THE PATTERN OF PROFITABLE
GROWTH IS TO BE CONTINUED IN THE FUTURE, THE
COMPANY MUST FIND A WAY TO EXPAND ITS SELLING
TERRITORIES AND AT THE SAME TIME INCREASE
SALES FROM PRESENT TERRITORIES WITHOUT
DISTURBING THE MORALE OF THE SALES FORCE.

PRESENT SITUATION   (2)
    CAN GROW 40% IN PRESENT FACILITIES
    NO FINANCIAL OBSTACLES TO FURTHER GROWTH

NECESSITY FOR GROWTH
    WHY? STAGNATION IS LINGERING DEATH
    REASONS: COSTS — INFLATION — NO GROWTH
             MEANS DECLINE

PROBLEMS
    CAN'T PUT MORE MEN IN PRESENT TERR.
    REASONS: LOW MORALE — MEN MIGHT QUIT —
             CAN'T GET MORE SALES FROM
             PRESENT FORCE — EXPLAIN

PUT MAP ON
V-GRAPH   ③

WHAT CAN WE DO?

PARKERSBURG – 86M – 1 MAN – DELIVERY PROBLEM
            UNECONOMIC
WHEELING – LOTS PEOPLE BUT – COMPETITION
    WASH – WEIRTON – PITT – PA
    STEUBENVILLE – OHIO
    ENTRENCHED – BIGGER THAN US – RISKY
            NO GO
MORGANTOWN – FAIRMONT – CLARKSBURG
250M – 3MEN
    DISADVANTAGE – DISTANCE – 2 DELIVERIES/WK
            COSTLY – BUT
    COULD BE PROFITABLE

SLOW
DOWN   ④

INSTITUTIONAL MEN
    1 HUNTINGTON
    1 BECKLEY/LOGAN

LOW ADDITIONAL DELIVERY COST – EXPLAIN
LITTLE CONFLICT WITH PRESENT SALESMEN
    EXPLAIN – DISCUSS

        SO

IF WE ADD 3 MEN M/F/C AND 2 INST MEN

    HOW DO WE COME OUT?
GO TO
EASEL   SHOW FIRST CHART

RECOMMENDATIONS

NOW YOU'RE BACK AT LECTERN.
SETTLE DOWN & DO A GOOD JOB READING
THIS.

SINCE THE PROJECTIONS, ALTHOUGH IN MY
OPINION CONSERVATIVE AND REALISTIC, APPEAR
SO FAVORABLE, I RECOMMEND WE ADD 1 SALESMAN
IN EACH OF THE CITIES OF MORGANTOWN,
FAIRMONT, AND CLARKSBURG AND 2 INSTITUTIONAL
SALESMEN, 1 IN HUNTINGTON AND 1 IN THE
BECKLEY/LOGAN AREA. I ALSO RECOMMEND THE
FOLLOWING ACTIONS BE ADOPTED TO PUT THE
PLAN INTO EFFECT.

---

⑥

COURSE OF ACTION -- SALESMEN
1, HIRE IN MORG
  2 WKS OFF AND WHSE - THEN
  2 WKS/SALSMN
  I'LL GET HIM STARTED
2, HIRE FOR FAIRMONT
  2 WKS BEHIND 1
  SAME PROGRAM
3, HIRE FOR CLARKSBURG
  2 WKS BEHIND #2   SAME DEAL

MEN SHOULD BE IN PRODUCTION 6 WEEKS AFTER
                       START

YOU'RE PROBABLY TALKING
TOO DAMN FAST

INSTITUTIONAL <u>MEN</u>   ⑦

    HIRE 1 FOR HUNTINGTON   NOW
         1 " BECKLEY/LOGAN   "
    1 MONTH OFFICE & WHSE TRAINING
    PLUS TIME IN FIELD WITH IN-HOUSE MAN
    <u>AND</u> TOP INST PRODUCER AMONG PRESENT
    SALESMEN

       IN PRODUCTION 6 WKS AFTER HIRE

GET READY FOR THE
        <u>CLOSE</u>

---

*PAUSE A FEW SECONDS. THIS IS FOR
              ALL THE MARBLES*
        <u>CLOSE</u>   ⑧

IN THE DEVELOPMENT OF THE PLAN I AM
PROPOSING TO YOU I HAVE CONSIDERED AND
ANALYZED EVERY FACT THAT APPEARS GERMANE
TO THE SITUATION; WHERE PROJECTION OR
ASSUMPTIONS HAVE BEEN MADE, I HAVE TESTED
EACH TO ASSURE IT IS SOUND AND REALISTIC.
IT IS MY BEST JUDGMENT THAT THE RECOMMENDED
COURSE OF ACTION WILL ENABLE OUR COMPANY
TO CONTINUE ITS PATTERN OF PROFITABLE
GROWTH.

      GOOD JOB, DAVE!

4

Other speech forms

If an executive is to consider himself a well-rounded speaker, he will not only master the art of preparing and delivering speeches and presentations but will also handle confidently a number of other speaking assignments. They may not be glamorous, but they are important in their own right, and a familiarity with a new set of principles is essential. The executive must learn to make a proper and seemly introduction, talk intelligently when called upon unexpectedly to address a meeting, control question and answer periods, speak fluently in informal company gatherings, be polite yet firm in one-on-one discussions.

Accordingly, let us spend a little time discussing these specialized speech forms.

INTRODUCTIONS

A good introduction is as rare as a perfect jewel, and the art of introducing a speaker properly is dying a lingering and unseemly death. There are reasons for this. The introducer either fails to understand the responsibilities of his function or is unwilling to accept the secondary supportive role he should assume. The man he introduces is the star of the show, but many introducers feel they deserve equal billing and that their performance is as eagerly awaited as the main event. Thus, instead of an introduction, they make a speech of their own, parading their oratorical talents and obtruding their personal beliefs on the subject the speaker will discuss.

How many times have you heard an introduction that either destroys the audience's receptiveness toward the speaker even before he opens his mouth, or makes it difficult for him to develop the mood he desires in his audience? The introducer who tells funny stories about the speaker or attempts to draw laughs at his expense is thrusting knives into his vitals. Consider the introducer who gleefully informs the audience that the speaker is the funniest man alive and will keep it in convulsions throughout his speech while the unfortunate object of his remarks grows angrier by the moment, since he is prepared to deliver a scholarly and extremely serious analysis of foreign trade problems.

Circumstances do affect situations, and introductions may vary in tone. At a dinner meeting of a group of people who are long-time friends, a certain levity is permitted, even desirable, when introducing a member of the group who is to speak. Liberties are the privilege of friendship, but this is not the case when an outsider is addressing an audience for the most part unknown to him. Here the occasion is formal and should be handled in a dignified manner.

In such a situation it is not unusual for a personal friend of the speaker to be asked to make the introduction. Many friendships have been shipwrecked on this reef. The introducer may have grown up next door to the member of the Supreme Court, but the justice may not enjoy the slightly off-color reference to the little blonde of uncertain morals who lived three houses down the street fifty years ago.

Preparing an introduction

The Honorable Henry Clay Pennypacker, senior senator from a midwestern state, has accepted an invitation to speak at the annual banquet of the Constitution Forever League at the Waldorf-Astoria. It will be a black tie affair. The president of the League, Hamilton Jackson, will perform the introduction of the senator, who will sit at his right during dinner.

Several weeks before the affair Jackson, who is somewhat of a wheel in his organization but does not know the senator personally, has an assistant gather material on him. *Who's Who* is an excellent source and so is the senator's office which forwards a three-page listing of the senator's accomplishments as well as biographical material. From this Jackson prepares a fulsome introduction and feels he is well prepared for his duty.

Not so. He has ignored the senator's possible wishes on the matter. He doesn't even know what to call the senator. Does he prefer to be addressed as Senator Henry Clay Pennypacker of Illinois or Indiana or whatever, or does he prefer an Honorable before his name and senator after it? Indeed, does he like to hear his full name or merely H. C. Pennypacker or even H. Clay Pennypacker? Little matters, but they may be and probably are important to the senator.

Hint:

□ Ask your speaker the exact form of his name you should use. Write it down and get it right.

Perhaps the senator is an egomaniac and wants every detail of his illustrious career mentioned in the introduction. On the other hand, it is possible he is intensely proud of the fact that he has recently been elected trustee of Siwash College, his alma mater, and would prefer that fact be headlined rather than a list of committees he has chaired during his twenty-two years in the Senate.

Hint:

    □ Ask the speaker what he would like you to say in your introduction. Do as he wishes. His will, not yours, should prevail.

        The title of the senator's speech may or may not have been made public. In either event Jackson should find out if he should mention or perhaps even comment on the subject.

Hint:

    □ Ask and obey the speaker's preference.

        Jackson's introduction should be short, concise. He should never lose sight of the fact that he is a spear carrier, a supernumerary, and under no circumstances should he attempt to upstage the star.

        He must never become afflicted with the "man who" political convention syndrome. All of us have suffered the misery of being exposed to an hour-long panegyric about a nameless hero, the man who did this, the man who did that, the man who will do so-and-so, and have been utterly unastonished to learn to our unsurprise that the man who will be the next president of the United States is none other than whosit.

Hint:

    □ The speaker who is being introduced has a name. Use it.

        All this is great, you say, but how does Jackson find out if his introduction will be approved by the senator? Good question. He starts by preparing an introduction from material he has assembled. It probably will not be possible for him to spend an hour privately with the senator who flies up from Washington in the afternoon, makes a short appearance at a special reception to meet the officers of the League and then is escorted by Jackson to the head table. During dinner, how-

ever, Jackson can go over with the senator what he plans to
say, seek the senator's comments and suggestions and make
necessary alterations to his introduction during dessert and
coffee. When the lectern and microphone are placed before
him, Jackson can rise, say, "Good evening, ladies and gentlemen. Our speaker tonight is Senator Pennypacker, and he has
chosen as his subject our country's current foreign policy.
Senator Pennypacker . . . ."

Jackson might not be the most polished speaker in the
world, yet he can be assured that in his introduction he will
say what the senator wants the audience to hear.

Despite his excellent start, Jackson has one serious hurdle
confronting him. How does he conclude his introduction?
Does he reach the end of his remarks and then in ringing
tones pronounce these immortal words, "And now, without
further ado, I give you Senator Pennypacker." I certainly
hope not. The senator might be no end of a chap, but it is a
sure bet there will be people in the audience who wouldn't
have him on a silver platter, and what the hell is this "ado"
business?

Hints:

□ If the title of the speech has already been mentioned, it need
not be repeated at this point. When the introduction has
been completed, Jackson pauses, then says, "Ladies and
gentlemen, Senator Pennypacker."

□ If the title has been saved until the end, the close is a bit
more involved. To word it this way is not good: "Ladies and
gentlemen, Senator Pennypacker, who will address us on . . . ."
The senator's name should come last. Thus: "The senator
will address us on . . . . Ladies and gentlemen, Senator Pennypacker."

□ If the speaker wishes to announce his subject himself, fine.
Ignore the matter and let him worry about it.

□ When Jackson has introduced the senator, he steps away from the lectern so the speaker can take his place. He moves his chair well back and away from the lectern and sits down.

□ At the end of the address Jackson moves back to the lectern and stands at the side of the senator. He says, "Thank you, Senator Pennypacker." No more, no less than that.

Making a few remarks—Formal occasions

The scene: the annual conference of the Constitution Forever League at the Boca Raton Club. The time: 12:20 P.M. The place: the large meeting hall with 429 men and women in attendance.

You have been somewhat inattentive to the speaker who has just finished his address. Your main concern for the past hour has been the malignant duck hook that has destroyed your game the last two days. You've been overswinging, and that egregious error coupled with the excessive speed of your backswing is the cause of your misery. If you can only slow the damn thing down, you'll get back your $28 this afternoon and could even come out with a net profit.

In the background you hear the chairman muttering something about a few minutes until lunch and would the head of the Committee for the Preservation of the First Amendment be good enough to make a few remarks to the League delegates on the progress of the committee.

It suddenly dawns on you that you are the committee chairman referred to, and it is you who is being called to the dais. Your first reaction, naturally, is that the meeting chairman is a sadistic, perverted so-and-so of a such-and-such.

The audience senses that you have been had. Your friends are sympathizing with you; your enemies gleefully look forward to your making an ass of yourself. Your golfing opponents are positive you will play even worse today, if that is possible. Your partner surreptitiously looks in his checkbook to determine how much he can afford to lose.

How do you confound your enemies, demonstrate to your friends that their solicitude, although welcome, is uncalled for? How do you seize victory from the ravening jaws of disaster?

What some of the audience expect you to do is stumble to the lectern, glower at the tormentor who has put you on the hot seat, mumble a few unintelligible words, and ignominiously flee. Others are prepared for you to rise, say, "No comment," and sit down. That is the abject craven's escape route. Neither of these paths is for you.

You leave your seat in the audience and walk slowly to the dais with a genial smile glued to your lips masking the murderous inclinations seething in your breast. Note that you walk slowly. There is a purpose to this: it gives you a few seconds to think. What are you thinking about? Your opening sentence—nothing else. At last you reach the lectern. The chairman has just finished telling the audience your name and affiliation. You bow politely to him, gaze calmly out at the sea of faces before you, and say, "I am delighted for this opportunity to tell you of the progress being made by our committee that is so deeply concerned with an issue vitally important to our country at the present moment."

You've met the challenge and are firmly in the saddle. True, the sentence was rather long. Also true, it didn't really say a great deal, but at least it sounded impressive. What comes next? It all depends on how your brain is functioning. If your committee has actually been making progress and if you can recall, at the moment, details of its activities, you may say a sentence or two about them. If your brain is not firing on all cylinders or if your committee, like most others, has been somnolent, inform your listeners that there is a great deal you would like to tell them, but you don't want to interfere with the luncheon arrangements. The purpose of this waffling is simply to give yourself time to work out a good closing sentence. Finally you get it. "You have the pledge of my committee," you say, "and I can't praise too much the devotion of the men and women who serve with me, that as soon as our deliberations are completed, we will place before you a fully developed plan of action for the League on this matter that is so important to every man, woman, and child in the country."

You smile for the last time to the audience, nod to the chairman, making the appropriate profane remarks sotto voce and leave the dais.

Bully for you! Again, the sentence was too damn long, but, what the hell, it rang with sincerity. You haven't said much; a critic listening to a recording of your remarks might conclude you said very little, and most of your conclusions had already been stated in your opening remark. The important fact is that you had been placed in an untenable, awkward situation and handled it with verve and aplomb.

You walk into lunch feeling virtuous and sorry for the vultures who picked your bones on the golf course the last two days. Today the stakes will be doubled. Your swing will be as smooth and unhurried as Gene Littler's.

Now, let us see what you have done, if not to achieve a triumph, at least to avert a disaster.

1. You have kept your cool even though some idiot called on you with no warning, which is a serious breach of professional ethics.
2. You quickly won the audience to your side since you remained calm despite feelings of irritation.
3. You moved slowly and deliberately enough to the lectern, so you had nearly a minute to get your first sentence lined up.

4. You talked for a couple of minutes after delivering your opening until you had time to work out your close.
5. When it was delivered, you stopped. (More on this later. It isn't as easy as it sounds.)

Hints:

- [ ] A good impromptu talk should never be more than three to five minutes in length.
- [ ] A strong opening is essential.
- [ ] A strong close is even more important.
- [ ] What comes between should be short and concise.
- [ ] When you have delivered your close, stop and keep silent from then on.
- [ ] Maintenance of sangfroid is helpful.
- [ ] So is a gracious and serene demeanor despite personal feelings of an entirely different quality.

Traps to avoid when making an impromptu talk

It might happen that an individual is called upon for a few unrehearsed remarks on a subject that is dear to his heart. He leaps to his feet, charges to the lectern, figuratively rolls up his sleeves, and flings wide the floodgates. Twenty minutes later there is no detectable abatement in the speed of his delivery or the flow of golden nuggets from his memory. The audience is stirring rebelliously, the chairman is wringing his hands and sweating profusely. He has only himself to blame.

Hint:

- [ ] Never ask for a few remarks from a person who has a reputation for verbosity.

Another type of impromptu speaker is the poor soul who starts well, says all that needs to be said, then doesn't know how to wrap it up and stop talking. He comes to the end of an appropriate closing sentence, suddenly remembers something too good not to mention, mentions it, closes again, remembers something else, closes still again, remembers, remembers, remembers . . . .

This is traumatic for the speaker, the audience, and the chairman who started it all.

Hints:

☐ Excise afterthoughts. Stop when you have come to your first close. Don't open your mouth again no matter what beautiful thought floats into your mind.

☐ Be conscious of elapsed time. Five minutes is the outside limit for impromptu remarks.

How can the chairman plug the Johnstown Dam once it is breached? This is not an easy assignment if the chairman has a reluctance to embarrass or anger a speaker who gets carried away with himself. Yet, the chairman does have an overriding obligation to the long-suffering audience.

Hint:

☐ When the speaker has continued clearly beyond the bounds of propriety, about the only option the chairman has is to be faster on his feet than the speaker. At the first opportune pause he springs forward with a gracious, "Thank you, Mr. Throckmorton, for your most perceptive remarks." He must be firm, forceful, and loud enough to drown out any further statements Mr. Throckmorton might wish to make.

Corporate short talks

Up to this point we have considered only impromptu remarks made in public or semipublic meetings. The executive discussing a problem with a group of peers in his own organization will often be called on for comments on the matter under discussion.

This form of communication has no relationship with what we have been considering. The corporate meeting is generally a give-and-take affair, interruptions are the rule rather than the exception, and each member of the group is expected to be thoroughly familiar with all facets of his department's involvement in the situation.

The senior member of the group will have no reluctance to stop an overlong monologue, and he will expect each person present to put forward his own views without having to be urged.

The rules controlling this type of meeting are loose, but there are obvious points that should be understood.

Hints:

- ☐ Be careful whom you interrupt and how you phrase your interruption.
- ☐ Learn when to talk and when to listen.
- ☐ Be perceptive of the impression you are making on the group.
- ☐ Keep your remarks short and to the point. Don't ramble.
- ☐ Remember that the man who can keep track of all the varying viewpoints that have been expressed and can wrap them into a conclusion that will be universally accepted has developed one of the most valuable talents required of top management.

Informal nonspeeches

For every hour the average executive spends in making formal speeches or presentations, he probably spends twenty hours delivering informal nonspeeches. As a matter of fact, the major portion of his working day is devoted to listening to or talking with others. They may be members of his own organization, customers, clients, bankers, lawyers, suppliers, or regulatory agencies. The list is endless. The discussions might be one-on-one, two-on-two, one-on-a-dozen, a dozen-on-one. Here again, the possible combinations are infinite.

There is a difference between addressing an audience of a hundred people and talking across a desk with a single individual. Yet, there are similarities between the two situations. The purpose of both might be to learn, to enlighten, to convince, to decide, or simply to explore a situation. Computers have been perfected to the point that they are almost human; technological advances in production methods are mind boggling; but nothing really happens until two or more people sit down, talk it over, and decide what to do.

Behaviorists have written hundreds of books on how people respond in a variety of stress and nonstress situations. They have reduced to a science the language of body movement; do you lean forward or back when talking, do you sit on the edge of your chair, are your legs crossed or not? Tone of voice holds no secrets for them, either. Is your manner aggressive, conciliatory? Will the words you use anger or please your listener? None of this is grist to our mill; we leave it to the experts in the field. There are, however, suggestions we do offer to executives concerned with the necessity of getting their jobs done in the most efficient way possible.

1. Courtesy. If the meeting is to be held in your office, your desk should be clear by appointment time and so should you. Your secretary should have been instructed to allow no interruptions during the meeting.

When your visitor arrives, you should rise, shake his hand if he is an outsider, and invite him to be seated.

Assuming both of you are busy men, no more than a minute or two should be spent in pleasantries, and then you, as the host, should introduce the subject of the meeting.

You should never forget that your visitor is your guest and is entitled to all the amenities he would receive were he visiting in your home.

2. Listening. In a meeting you should spend more time listening than you do talking. The art of being a good listener does not come naturally to most of us and should be deliberately and consciously developed.

Hints:

- □ Do not interrupt a speaker.
- □ Do not hog the conversation.
- □ Do not show signs of impatience even if you are denied equal time to contribute your two cents' worth. Your chance will come.
- □ If another talker can't find a word, don't prompt him. Let him stumble around until he finds it.
- □ Do not show signs of inattention. What he is saying may be very important to a speaker even though you do not see the relevance of his remarks.

A digression on hearing versus listening

There is a vast distinction between the words. In the Navy it is: "Now hear this." A mother wearily admonishing her child says: "Pay attention, dear." The unfortunate fact is that instructions or pearls of wisdom often go in one ear and out the other. The foursome gathered in the 19th hole after the game is not usually a quiet group. Its members, if reasonably sober, do not always interrupt a speaker, but the silent three are not listening to the words of the fourth. They are mentally rehearsing how they will describe the masterful chip from the base of the azalea bush that earned a miraculous half at the crucial point in the match.

Hearing is one thing; paying attention to what is said is quite another. It is surprising what one can learn if one really listens. Try it sometime.

Nothing flatters a speaker more than the knowledge that the audience is hanging on every word uttered. The disinterested person is being unconsciously rude, and if he doesn't pay attention to what I am saying, why should I concern myself with his silly blathering? Be careful whom you offend by obvious inattention. Perhaps your friends bore you because they never say anything worth listening to. No harm done. Your utterances are undoubtedly equally boring to them.

But, don't let the boss sense you are hearing him rather than listening to what he has to say. Your inattention could be a costly mistake.

Now, a further digression on listening. Five minutes after you are introduced to four strangers, do you remember their names? Recalling one or at the most two is probably average. You console yourself by admitting that as you grow older your memory becomes less and less dependable. Absolute rot! If you put your mind to it, you can recall accurately every one of the ninety-three strokes you used on the golf course last Saturday. Five days against five minutes, ninety-three blows against four names.

Memory has nothing to do with it. You were paying attention to what you were doing when you were chasing the elusive ball, and you were hearing rather than listening when the introductions were made.

So, pay attention when you meet strangers. Repeat names aloud when you hear them and say them three or four more times to yourself. Memory is not the culprit; lack of attention is.

3. Maintaining unfailing good humor. The quickest way to lose the battle is to lose your temper. If the other chap gets hot under the collar, that's his loss. Don't respond with a similar degree of warmth.

Hints:

- □ Resolve beforehand to keep your cool even though your vis-à-vis is a goader of repute. Stick to your resolve, come what may.
- □ Don't be hard to get along with. Having a reputation of irascibility can be a severe handicap for an executive on the way up.
- □ Refuse to be drawn into an open confrontation.
- □ Don't force your opponent into a corner from which he must come out swinging. Always leave an escape hatch.

4. *Analytical judgment.* It is important to realize that you may not always be right. It is important to recognize that another person may be as competent and as knowledgeable as you are. He could be right, and you could be wrong.

Hints:

- □ Don't box yourself in by being too cocky, too dogmatic, too bellicose.
- □ Show a willingness to concede if it seems right or politic to do so.

5. *Attitude when operating under specific orders.* A situation might arise that requires you to be firm and unyielding on a specific point. When such an issue arises, you should make your statement as pleasantly as possible and let it be known that you are unable to negotiate on the point. This does not prevent you from paying close attention to the arguments advanced to counter your stand, nor does it prevent you from taking careful note of them so they can be set forth accurately to your principals.

Hint:

- □ Instructions to take an unyielding stand on an issue do not mean you cannot listen to an opposing view. To the contrary, the firmer your stand the more willing you should be to hear arguments against it, first having made clear you are powerless to alter your position.

6. *Level of behavior.* Under no circumstances should you ever lower your standard of manners. If the air around you is fogged with "he don't," "I ain't," "you know," coarse expressions or four letter words, don't join in. There is no more reason for you to lower your standards of speech than there is for you to come to the meeting clad in a dirty shirt and no necktie.

Hint:

□ Be yourself. Never slide down to a lower level in speech, manners, or attitude.

Questions and answers

It is not at all unusual for the chairman of a meeting to announce that at the end of a presentation there will be a short period in which the audience may ask questions of the speaker. There is much a speaker can do to make the session a success. Conversely, there is ample opportunity for disaster to strike.

For example, a speaker concludes the presentation, the chairman thanks him and asks for questions. None are forthcoming and the speaker stands, uncomfortable and helpless while the audience squirms uneasily. Should this happen, the speaker is paying for failure to plan properly.

Hints:

□ Before he begins his speech, he can plant the first question with the chairman who, as soon as he opens the question period, feeds it smoothly back to the speaker. Once the ice is broken, other questions should flow spontaneously.

☐ He can arrange with a friend in the audience to ask the first question. He will choose a subject he is reasonably sure he can handle effectively. He should be careful to pick a stooge who could be relied on to be present and awake when the time comes for him to pose his question.

☐ He can start the session by asking himself a question. "Many of you have been wondering how..." he commences and then goes on to give the answer.

☐ He may ask the audience a question. This is an effective way to develop a lively session, especially if the question he poses relates to an issue on which feelings run high. A speaker must be prepared to ride the whirlwind he foments should his question be so controversial it precipitates a verbal brawl.

☐ If a speaker is left on his own without a chairman to protect him, he must exercise firm control so that a half dozen individuals are not competing for air time at the same moment.

☐ He must be prepared to deal summarily with a member of the audience who wishes to make a speech of his own.

☐ If a question period is lively and time is running out, the speaker should announce he will be able to accept only one more question. Don't let it drag on and on.

Good question and answer sessions don't just happen. They are planned as carefully as good speeches are planned. In addition, they require a firm hand on the tiller. Some questions will not be germane to the subject of the speech. Others may be so specialized that they have little interest for the majority of the audience. In a press conference the president can avoid an issue he doesn't wish to discuss by saying a few words and then pointing to another questioner. The

102

average speaker cannot act in such an arbitrary fashion, yet he cannot allow a persistent questioner to spoil a session.

Most questions will be reasonable and asked in a friendly manner. If they are not relevant, the speaker can sidestep them gracefully without offending the person who poses them.

Hints:

- Don't waste time on irrelevant issues.
- An arbitrary attitude on the part of the speaker encourages a similar attitude in the audience.
- Be courteous in your answers at all times.
- Be especially gracious when you duck a question.

If a single individual in an audience digs in and won't desist in an attempt to turn questions and answers into an argument, he must be handled politely but with resolution.

Hint:

- Smile at him. Say, "It looks as if we don't agree on this point. Rather than take the time of the whole group why don't we meet in the bar at six o'clock and discuss it further." The odds are ten to one he'll never show.

This ploy is known as isolating the opposition. It is an effective way of getting a man off your back as it leaves him no reason to attempt to continue a private argument in public.

There is another type of questioner who is never satisfied with an answer but always counters with a further question.

Hint:

- When you are the target of such a basilisk, never be looking at him when you complete your answer. Be looking somewhere else and pick a new question as quickly as possible from a different sector of the audience.

In general, although a question comes from an individual, the answer should be made to the entire audience.

Hint:

- □ Do not maintain eye contact with the questioner as you give your answer. Ignoring this precept may involve you in a one-on-one discussion which should always be avoided, if possible.

Finally, some questions may be difficult to answer and require reflection on the part of the speaker before committing himself.

Hint:

- □ When a question is a tough one, always repeat it, ostensibly to make sure all the audience has heard it. This gives the speaker a few seconds to think about the answer before he delivers it.

Many experienced question answerers repeat all questions. This is the ultraconservative approach and cannot be faulted, but when a simple query is posed in clear, belllike tones, repetition is unnecessary redundancy.

Allowing questions during a speech

On occasion, a speaker might suggest that the audience ask questions or request clarification of a point during the course of his speech. He does this in a misguided effort to be helpful to his listeners. What can happen as a result?

1. The audience takes off in a direction not anticipated and refuses to be brought to heel.

2. The speaker never gets to number two of the eleven points he intended to make.

3. His well-prepared speech is a shambles.

Hints:

☐ Never give your audience an opportunity to interrupt your speech.

☐ Tell the audience if there are questions you will be happy to answer them at the conclusion of your talk.

☐ In an attempt to be a nice guy, don't destroy your speech and make an ass of yourself.

☐ Remember that most audiences contain at least one sadist whose principal aim in life is to disembowel a speaker. Don't play into his hands by presenting him with a well-honed scalpel.

5

Putting it together

Now, dear reader, we have, I hope, traveled companion ably through the mysteries of researching a speech or presentation, preparing it and its exhibits, and then delivering it to a live audience. We have one more individual to add to our company of performers. Timothy Golightly is a worthy companion to the sales manager, the banker, the "few remarks" man, and the introducer whom we have already met and in whom we have, perhaps, discovered some characteristics that remind us of ourselves.

An opportunity has been given us to see an exact transcript of the words spoken by Golightly in a rehearsal of a speech he must soon make and to read the unquestionably acerbic comments of the chairman of his company written after he had attended the practice run. I can imagine that Golightly was considerably dismayed by the sharpness of his boss's criticism, but I hope he is intelligent enough to profit from it.

Golightly is the newly appointed president of Monarch Systems, a company engaged in selling computer time and leasing computer machinery. Monarch has had a history of inconsistent performances, and last year's substantial loss has resulted in the replacement of the former president by Golightly.

The company has been in business for eight years, and in that time sales have grown to $14 million. Each year management has predicted substantial earnings due to increased sales, but something usually happened that reduced actual earnings far below projections. The results of the previous year came as a complete surprise to management. As late as December the company was looking forward to earnings in excess of $400,000, but the auditors discovered a serious overstatement in book value of rental equipment and a large inventory shortage. Adjustments changed the expected profit to a loss of $250,000.

The choice of Golightly as president was based on his strong financial background and the reputation he had made as a financial officer of another computer company. Monarch's sales curve was excellent, but unless improvement was achieved in the control functions, the company could not expect to survive. The new president had been hired in late January. It is now early April, and the annual meeting of the company's stockholders will be held at a local hotel in three weeks.

Golightly has had little experience in speaking, but the chairman has informed him that he would be expected to address the stockholders. Ordinarily, no more than forty or fifty people attended the meeting. This year it was expected that a greater number would appear because of the disappointing loss incurred the previous year despite the glowing projections of the former president. It was probable that the stockholders in attendance would not be kindly disposed toward management.

Golightly did not enjoy the prospect of facing such an audience. He was new on the job and not responsible for what had happened in the past. To top it off, he was not a polished speaker. In addition, since this book had not yet been published, there was practically no place he could go for professional advice on the preparation and delivery of his speech.

Yet, Golightly did not despair. After all, a man who became president of a reasonably large corporation at the age of thirty-seven must have a lot of ability. So it was that Golightly went about his assignment in a confident frame of mind. He decided what he wanted to cover in his speech, outlined it, and then began his preparation. Ten days before the meeting he staged a dress rehearsal to an audience composed of the chairman, two outside directors, and three senior officers of the company. Top management realized the importance of the new president's first report to the stockholders and wanted to be sure he made the best possible impression. Another disaster might have serious effects on the company or even sweep the present management out of office. That would never do!

Golightly's speech, which was short, was videotaped so that later he could watch himself as he delivered it. When he finished, Tim looked at Justin Lodge, the chairman, for some indication of how he had done. Lodge was giving nothing away.

"Could be worse for starters," he said, "but your act needs a lot of cleaning up. I'll have a transcript prepared, make my notes, and get it all back to you by Friday so you can rewrite and rehearse over the weekend. We'll have another run-through on Monday. In the meantime, watch and listen to yourself. Talk to the others as well, but don't forget you are president of this outfit, and you take orders only from me."

Lodge brushed the cigar ashes from his vest and walked slowly from the room. It was difficult to read his mind, and Golightly was uncertain as to his reaction to the speech he had heard. Nor was he sure how he would assess his own performance. The reaction of the other listeners did not appear to be ecstatic. Tim was not encouraged by their rather glum faces, but he would do what Lodge had suggested. The prospect of receiving the chairman's notes comforted him, but at the same time left him with a feeling of foreboding.

On the appointed day Tim received a sheaf of papers from Lodge. The pages contained a transcript of his words and Lodge's comments.

> Ladies and Gentlemen:
> A few weeks ago you, uh, received a copy of the annual report covering the operations of your company in the year ended this, I beg your pardon, last December 31. The bottom line was, uh, a severe disappointment to you as it was to the management.

To: T. Golightly
From: J. Lodge
Subject: Annual Meeting Speech

I'll give you a good introduction. Since this is your first public appearance, don't you think you should say something about how you feel about the company and your job?

Get rid of the "uhs." (Two)

Don't apologize for a slip of the tongue. Correct yourself and keep going.

"Bottom line"—don't use phrases like this in a formal speech.

Your opening must be strong and delivered accurately. Write out first couple of sentences. Beef them up.

Watch yourself on tape. Don't stand so stiffly. Look at the audience.

> The causes of the loss were explained in the report, and I will not dwell on them any further at this point in time. Later, other members of (the) management (team) and I will attempt to answer your questions. At present, however, I feel it is, uh, more important to tell you about the financial status of your company as it is today, what we have done to prevent similar mistakes in the future and, uh, uh, what we can look for in the future.

Good concept—just the right touch. No sense in flogging a dead horse. A good talk from you here will make questions more civil. Get stockholders thinking of the future, not the past. But you must express yourself better.

Eliminate words in parentheses.

"Attempt to answer questions." Hell, you better be able to answer them.

Three more "uhs." "At this point in time" NO!, NO! "At this time" or even better, "now." Get your head up from your notes. Don't clutch the lectern in an iron grip. "Future" twice. Rephrase.

Your company is solvent and viable. We are taking discounts on the payment of current bills, and our bankers have expressed their, uh, confidence by extending a $3 million revolving line of credit to us secured by a lien on our receivables. Our current ratio is 1.6 to 1 and our acid test ratio is .8, both, uh, uh, excellent figures.

"Viable" NO!!

Your audience will not be a group of CPAs. Will they understand revolving lines of credit, current ratios, and acid tests? I doubt it. Keep it simple. Rephrase.

Three more "uhs."

Idea behind this paragraph good. The patient is alive and doing well. Now, get this idea across in terms that will appeal to the nonfinancial stockholder.

You are teetering from one foot to the other. Get your left hand out of your pocket and leave your damn necktie alone.

For the last three months my efforts have been oriented in the direction of improving the accounting policies and practices of your company and inventory controls have been completely overhauled and an entirely new system has been implemented and is now operative.

> Basic intent good.
> "Oriented" Out!
> "Implemented" Out!
> "Operative" Out!
> Talk to the audience, not down to your notes. Let note cards lie on the lectern. Don't wave them in your hand.
> Four "ands" in this collection of clauses and phrases. Talk in sentences. Don't run on and on, and on.

Control over depreciation and depreciated values of rental equipment has been strengthened and no substantial variation is possible at the time of the next audit and in addition, studies are now, uh, uh, underway in other areas of our control function and I am absolutely confident that our treasury department will operate at a substantially higher degree of efficiency and at the same time payroll and administrative costs in this area will be reduced by a minimum of, uh, 20 percent by year-end.

> You better be right on this statement.
> Three more "uhs."
> "No substantial variation is possible . . . ." "I am absolutely confident . . . ." I'm glad you feel this way, but your words are vividly reminiscent of statements often made by your predecessor. I hope the parallel will not be extended. Temper your enthusiasm. Vehemence of rhetoric does not add validity to statements.
> Cut payroll by 20 percent sounds good to stockholders, but what will union officers' reaction be? Might be wise to say nothing about this.
> You are starting to talk very rapidly and are slurring word endings. Watch this and slow it down. Your hair looks great. LEAVE IT ALONE!!!
> Blockbuster sentence. Cut out the "ands" and break it up.

The scenario for the balance of the year in financial matters is efficiency combined with lower costs.

Scenarios have to do with movies. Why not say what your "objective" is?

Your company is now profitable. I am pleased to (be able to) announce that in the first quarter of the current year your company made a profit of $197,000. These figures are (of course), unaudited, but I would stake my reputation on their accuracy. No provision has been made for income taxes as the carry-forward credit for last year's loss gives us a cushion of $250,000 before it will be necessary to accrue taxes.

(Eliminate)
"Your company" twice in one sentence. Change. $197,000 is a figure, not "figures."
Here you go, staking your reputation again. Your *job* is on the line. If you lose it, your reputation is gone too. Stop making statements like this. Whole paragraph without an "uh." Progress! Hand and arm movements still stiff. Please keep your head up and look at the audience.

Now, what about the rest of the year? I have had a (simple) chart prepared to show projected results, uh, uh, and how they compare with last year. These projections are based on our best judgment of what we expect for the period. Of course, nothing is certain these days and the state of our national economy, international trade balances, political unrest throughout the world and even unfavorable legislation by Congress can impact our estimates. However, we believe they are realistic and feasible. Hopefully they can be attained.

Two "uhs."
(Eliminate)
This chronicle of possible disasters—why doesn't it include a total

Arab oil embargo, California sliding into the Pacific, China and the Reds forming an alliance? Is all this really necessary or germane? If we blow it again, it'll be entirely our fault, and you'll be fall guy number one.

"Impact." Horrible. "Affect." Impact is a noun and don't forget it.

"Hopefully." What the hell does that mean? Where did you learn all these disgusting words? Forget them.

Either stay at the lectern while you finish what you are saying, or go to the easel and talk there. Don't wander around addressing the floor.

MONARCH SYSTEMS

	CURRENT YEAR ESTIMATE	LAST YEAR ACTUAL
GROSS REVENUES	$ 15,200,000	$ 14,026,000
EXPENSES	14,450,000	14,276,000*
INCOME BEFORE TAXES	750,000	(250,000)
PROVISION FOR TAXES	260,000**	————
NET INCOME	$ 490,000	($ 250,000)
EARNINGS PER SHARE	$ .61***	($ .31)

* INCLUDES $400,000 EXTRAORDINARY AND NON-RECURRING EXPENSE.
** REDUCED $122,000 AS A RESULT OF NET LOSS CARRY-FORWARD
*** BASED ON 801,000 SHARES OUTSTANDING.

You will note that sales are projected to increase by about $1,200,000 or almost 8 percent. Mr. Hendricks, vice president of sales, will give you his input on this later. Expenses, giving effect to changes already implemented and others on the drawing board, are budgeted at $14,450,000, up only 1 percent. This will result in profits after taxes of almost $500,000 or $0.61 per share. To date, our most profitable year was 1976 when we earned $0.31 per share.

A good exhibit, but are all three footnotes necessary? Make as simple as possible so stockholders will see only what is essential. Cover the rest in your remarks.

Don't talk to the easel—it doesn't give a damn what you say. The stockholders do.

Don't stand in front of the easel. We can't see through you.

When you finish with the chart, cover it and walk back to the lectern before you open your mouth again.

No "uhs" in this section. What happened? Find out and do whatever it is all through your speech.

Hendricks will *not* give his "input" later. He will discuss his sales projections.

"Implemented" again. Please.

"On the drawing board." You are a financial man, not an architect.

Ladies and gentlemen, that concludes my remarks. Mr. Hendricks will now tell you about prospects in the leasing and service divisions. When he has completed his presentation, we will be ready to, uh, uh, to accept questions from the floor. Thank you.

You have already referred to what Hendricks will say. Tell them once and once only.

Two "uhs." Damn—that makes a total of fifteen. Reduce to zero.

"Accept questions from the floor." A term frequently used but consider, for a moment, what the words actually mean. Why not, "answer your questions"? Have you ever regarded simplicity as a virtue?

One important point. Your story basically is:

1. Things have been bad.
2. We have done this and that to turn company around.
3. Things will be much better.

This is smart—get away from the past. Concentrate on the future. You wind up projecting the best year in history of the company.

This gives you an opportunity to romance on the future. Why not take it? You are trying, or should be, to establish your personality and competence with the stockholders—this is the first time they have seen you. Take them by the hand for a short stroll down the garden path. Sell yourself and the company.

Think this over. Whatever you do, you better be right. We have had all the surprises we want for the next ten years. Whatever close you decide on, make it strong. Write it out and deliver it firmly.

Your lead-in for Hendricks is good.

You took almost exactly five minutes to make this talk. You need to slow your delivery somewhat. With suggested changes and additions I should think your actual presentation will run seven or eight minutes. Just about right.

Work on this over the weekend. Practice, rehearse.

See you Monday.

Note: I have listened to and watched you once again. You act and come across as a rather rigid, stiff individual—not wholly at ease and lacking in self-confidence. This is understandable. You must be yourself—no argument about that—but try to get away from the green eyeshade figure filbert image and act more like the president of a good-sized company. Ease—smoothness—work on it. Know what you are talking about, say it right, show it clearly.

Good luck,

J. L.

Transition

The saga of Timothy Golightly concludes the first part of this book. Incidentally, he did a very creditable job on his speech to the stockholders, and I am happy to state that Monarch Systems is now surpassing management's profit expectations.

So much for speaking. Now a few words on the writing section that follows. Before we go into that, however, permit me to digress for a moment. Somewhere in the archives of Harvard repose the notes Churchill prepared for one of his major speeches. A word or two sufficed to remind him of points he wished to make, but all his transitions were fully written out. He must have considered the wrap-up of what he had been saying on one subject and the introduction of the next to be critical parts of his speech.

If Sir Winston attached such importance to his transitions, I should attempt to emulate his example. Although there are great differences between speaking and writing, they have much in common. Both means of communication use words and are strengthened by proper grammar, syntax, and sentence construction. Both require clarity, succinctness, and total honesty. Thorough analysis and preparation are essential to both arts. Above all, writing and speaking must be convincing.

So, much that has been said on speaking is valid for writing, and the reverse is equally true. I suppose the main difference between speaking and writing is this: the spoken word is reinforced by tone, emphasis of voice, gestures, body movements, and visual contact with the audience, while the written work relies wholly on the words it contains. On the other hand, few presentations are recorded and available for a rerun, while a report can be read a dozen times.

Because of these differences, a written message must be different from a spoken one. The following chapters will be concerned with the principles that apply more specifically to writing.

6

The use and misuse of words

The wise writer knows the meaning of the words he uses. If he is not certain he has chosen the right word, he checks it in the dictionary. Should he be unable to find it, he should realize that the word does not exist or he is not spelling it correctly. Either conclusion warrants the choice of a different word.

Mrs. Malaprop was a mistress of the art of picking the wrong word for the right occasion. She had a knack of using a word that sounded almost like the one she should have selected. For two centuries theatergoers have chuckled at "like an allegory on the banks of the Nile," but how many corporate presidents chuckle when they read the minutes of a directors' meeting and find that "the meeting was *adjoined* at four o'clock"? Have you ever seen an ad in the Help Wanted section of the newspaper that starts: "Stock Clerk— High *Renumeration*"?

Here are a few more tricky pairs of words:

Accept—Receive.	Except—Everything else but.
Affect—Influence.	Effect—To bring to pass (verb), result (noun).
Allude—Make indirect reference to.	Elude—Avoid adroitly, escape.
Appraise—To evaluate.	Apprise—To give notice, tell.

117

118

Capital—Capital letter. Capital assets. Principal. City serving as seat of government. Part of a column. Capitalism.

Capitol—A building in which a state legislature meets or in which the U.S. Congress meets.

The House and the Senate meet in the *capitol* (that big building on the hill) at the *capital* (Washington).

Compliment—An expression of esteem, respect, a flattering remark.

Complement—To complete, make perfect.

Farther—Refers to distance.

Further—Refers to time or quantity.

Imply—Suggest indirectly.

Infer—Draw meaning from data.

I infer from your implication that . . .

It's—Contraction of *it is*.

Its—Possessive of *it*.

It's a thrill to hear a bird sing *its* song.

Less—Refers to quantity.

Fewer—Refers to number.

Fewer people have learned to talk *less*. An unclear but fascinating concept.

May—Permission granted. You *may* take a leave. Perhaps, uncertainty. I *may* take a leave.

Can—Implies physical ability to take an action.

Principle—A basic rule or truth.

Principal—Number one in rank. Capital as distinguished from spending money.

Verbal—Using words, written or spoken.

Oral—Uttered by mouth.

Adjectives

Picking the right adjective can be a problem. According to the grammarians an adjective is a word serving as a modifier of a noun to denote a special quality of the thing named, to indicate its quantity or extent, or to differentiate a thing from something else.

Examples of the three types of adjectives:

A *famous* man

A *full* cup

The *fourth* son

No problem so far, but what about choosing the proper adjective to convey the writer's precise meaning? Take the familiar word *famous*. It is a catchall with a number of more specific synonyms that can be used to capture the exact meaning in the mind of the writer. For instance:

Famous—(*a*) widely known, (*b*) honored: an unspecific general word.

Celebrated—Implies more notice and attention, especially in print: a *celebrated* actor.

Renowned—Implies more glory and acclamation: a *renowned* author.

Noted—Suggests well deserved public attention: a *noted* authority.

Notorious—Adds an implication of questionableness or evil: the *notorious* Jesse James.

Distinguished—Implies excellence or superiority: the *distinguished* judge.

Eminent—Greater than distinguished.

Illustrious—Implies enduring honor and glory attached to a deed or person: Thomas Lincoln's *illustrious* son.

To call Abe Lincoln *notorious* or Jesse James *illustrious* would be improper. We are told that Winston Churchill, in writing a speech, changed one adjective eleven times before he found the one that expressed his exact meaning.

Poets and writers of flowery prose use adjectives to add color and imagery to their writing. Authors of business communications should be restrained so they will not allow their rhetoric to carry them away. From our childhood days we

have sung "... by the dawn's early light ...." *Early* is redundant. What other kind of light could the dawn provide?

The business writer should use as few adjectives as possible. The major trouble is that most of them are imprecise and
convey no exact meaning. Take this sentence: "Pin-Up Corporation expects to earn _____ profit this year." Fill in the
blank with one of the following adjectives, adding an article
if necessary:

Acceptable	Low
Adequate	Nominal
Appropriate	Reasonable
Average	Slight
High	Small
Inadequate	Some
Large	Substantial
Little	Unacceptable

Each adjective may have a different shade of meaning from
all the others, but the reader is forced to make the decision as
to what the word means to him. No two readers can be expected to agree on the definition of what is *adequate*.

If the writer expects Pin-Up to earn $850,000, let him say
so and allow the reader to decide if this amount is *adequate,
substantial, reasonable,* or whatever. Of course, the writer
who commits himself to a precise figure must answer to the
consequences if he proves to be wrong, but he is paid to be
right and should not be allowed to shirk his responsibility by
using weasel words. Avoid the use of vague modifiers; always
be as specific as you can.

Foreign words and phrases

Don't spice your writing with an overabundance of foreign
words or phrases. They sound ostentatious and should be used

only when there is no equal substitute in standard English.

An *ad hoc* committee is one formed to perform a single specific service. The president of a company may be, *ex officio,* a member of a company committee. In other words, his membership is due to his position.

Both of these Latin phrases are acceptable as they have become familiar to most of us, and it is difficult to coin an equivalent, concise English phrase.

There is a very real distinction between Americanized foreign words and those that still maintain their foreign flavor. Only the latter group should be avoided in business writing. Examples of Americanized foreign words:

Détente
Delicatessen
Matinee
Résumé

Other words are familiar to most of us; some of them have been Americanized, but they still sound foreign. Since there are even more familiar substitutes we can use, we should choose them in preference to the foreign word. Examples:

Don't write	*When you mean*
Bête noir	Bugbear.
Bona fide	Authentic, sincere, in good faith.
Caveat emptor	Let the buyer beware.
En route	On the way.
Faux pas	Blunder.
Gratis	Free.
Naïve	Artless, credulous, natural.
Nouveau riche	New rich.
Parvenu	Upstart.
Raison d'être	Reason for existence.
Sine qua non	Essential thing.

The phrase *hors d'oeuvres* is in a class of its own. It conjures up a vision of caviar, red and black, smoked salmon, artichoke hearts, anchovies coiled on melba toast, and all sorts of delicacies. *Appetizer* is a pallid substitute, but I suggest that in conversation, at least, you stay with *appetizer* until you are absolutely certain of your pronunciation of *hors d'oeuvres*.

Words flow back and forth across oceans and frontiers, and in the course of time become citizens of the countries they invade. Consider these words:

Chassis	Garage
Chauffeur	Landau
Coupe	Limousine
Detour	Tonneau

One might almost suspect the automobile had been invented in France rather than in Detroit.

A good rule to follow with regard to foreign words and phrases is to use them only if they have been Americanized or if there is no readily available substitute in American English.

Businessese

Young executives attempt to impress their peers and especially their superiors by their mastery of a vocabulary composed of what, in business schools, are called *buzz words*. Many of these are excellent words when properly used, but most of them are pallid substitutes for words better suited to the purpose. A few are colorful and descriptive. For example, *bottom line,* meaning the end result, is more pleasing to the ear than the *net, net* it is in the process of replacing. Yet, Thomas Jefferson did not say that the *bottom line* was "life, liberty, and the pursuit of happiness."

Implement as a verb is much overused. The dictionary does dignify its use, but when policies, programs, actions, and practices are *implemented* a half dozen times a page, the reader feels he has been bludgeoned with a blunt implement and has been exposed to the inane ramblings of an ignoramus.

So many *scenarios* are being *orchestrated* in business communications, one might feel all corporations are engaged in fitting musical accompaniments to filmed epics.

Enterprising authors are now marketing books containing lists of hundreds of jargon words with which bosses will be impressed, and aspiring executives are being told that fluency in this new language is a prerequisite for a successful career. Ridiculous.

At some point in time has been an enduring favorite of the aficionados of businessese. I presume we are to visualize time as extending from here to there, and if we make a mark with a pencil between the two limits (parameters to some misguided souls), we have established *some point in time.* Why not say *at some time* or *when?*

Impact, improperly used as a verb, is another favorite of the jargoneers. *Impact* is a good verb; it means to fix fairly, to press together, or to impinge upon. Agreed, but it is not proper to say, "Rising costs will impact profits." Rising costs will *reduce, affect,* or *lower* profits; they will never *impact* them.

Here is a short list of businessese words. More are being coined daily, and you should feel free to make continuing additions. An occasional use of some of them is not a heinous crime, but overuse is to be avoided.

Bottom line	Feedback	Input
Challenging	Frame of reference	Interface
Dialogue	Hopefully	Linkage
Dichotomy	Implement (v.)	Meaningful

Orchestrate	Rewarding	Thrust
Output	Scenario	Track record
Parameter	Synergy	Value judgment
Relevant	Throughput	Viable

Gobbledygook

When convoluted syntax and tortuous sentence structure are superimposed on a plethora of businessese jargon, the result is gobbledygook.

This word is found in dictionaries and can be defined as "wordy and generally unintelligible jargon." Its spawning ground is the swampy wastes of barren bureaucratic cranial vacuums. (Not bad as an example of amateur gobbledygook.) As far back as World War II a blackout order was phrased this way: "Obscure fenestration with opaque coverings or terminate the illumination." It would never do to have said: "Pull down the shades or turn out the lights." In a simpler vein, when an aspirant threw his hat into the presidential ring, a commentator referred to the act as a "meaningful threshold for a viable campaign."

Here is an example of gobbledygook in its most advanced and purest form. "It has been decisioned," wrote the commandant of the Marine Corps, "that some form of unit rotation may be a desirable objective .... Recent CMC decisions have alleviated the major inhibitors allowing a fresh approach and revaluation of alternative methods of unit replacement . . . ."

I object to: *decisioned.* What's wrong with *decided?*

I object to: *may be a desirable objective.* The CMC should be capable of deciding whether it was or wasn't desirable. CMCs, I hope, are men of action, not wafflers.

I object to: *alleviated the major inhibitors.* Why not *made it possible?*

I object to: *fresh approach and revaluation.* Redundant. Why not *review?* (One positive note: the CMC did not write re-evaluation.)

What regulation would the CMC have violated had he written: "It is now possible and desirable to review various methods of unit replacement." I hope the CMC did not close his statement with a request to be *copied* with all *interreactions* to his directive.

Strive for clarity. Don't use long words when short ones will do the job better.

Don't use	*When you can use*
Circumvent	Avoid
Defunct	Dead, out of business
Eternal vigilance	Alertness
Forfeit	Lose
Increment	Growth, increase
Minimal	Least
Parameter	Limit, bound
Periphery	Rim
Peruse	Look over
Preponderant	Chief
Rescind	Call off
Subsequently	Later
Unavailability	Lack of
Unequivocal	Certain
Utilization	Use

Use of Latin abbreviations

Suggestion: Don't use them.
Exception: When clearly superior to alternatives.
Example: Dodgers v. Giants. It is not easy to find a suitable substitute for *v.*

Don't use	When you can use
cf.	compare
e.g.	for example
et al.	and others
etc.	and so forth
i.e.	that is
re or in re	about, concerning
viz	namely

Clichés

I have a happy recollection of Jimmy Demaret doing a TV commentary on a golf match some years ago. As I remember, he said something like this: "Jack, wielding his trusty Texas wedge, canned a snake from the froghair." Sports heroes have been known to tarnish their images when they open their mouths. Baseball players are no exception to this generalization. How often have you heard the slugging outfielder say: "He'd been tossing up junk and breaking stuff, you know, but I waited for his high hard one, and when it came, uh, I went with the pitch, got good wood on it and rode it to the opposite field seats, you know what I mean." In other words he hit it *good*.

Practicing athletes and jock broadcasters who have been boning up on Ring Lardner are not the only murderers of the King's English. Businessmen are equally bitten by the cliché bug. Instead of a stale cliché, use a fresh, direct word.

Cliché	Substitute
As a matter of fact	Leave it out entirely.
Explore every avenue	Analyze.
In accordance with	By, following.
In most cases	Usually.

Cliché	Substitute
In the last analysis	Excise the whole phrase.
On the grounds that	Because.
Strive with might and main	Try.
The foreseeable future	The future (who can foresee the future?).
To my knowledge and belief	I know.
To tell the truth	Redundant. We assume you always tell the truth.
To the best of my ability	Forget it. We assume everything you do is to the best of your ability.
With the result that	So that.

Slang

There is no place for slang in business writing. Prose can be dignified without being pompous or stilted. Individuals should never be referred to as *this guy* or *that fellow. Ain'ts* should be reserved for dialogue in short stories.

Going down the tube, meaning approaching bankruptcy, is a colorful expression but more fitted to a business school classroom than to a business communication.

Today, when we are *between a rock and a hard place,* we stoically *bite the bullet.* Reserve such histrionics for describing your emotions as you reach for your wallet after blowing a six-foot putt on the last green to lose the match.

Jokes, coarseness, and profanity should be avoided in formal writing. The person you offend may be the one individual you can't afford to upset.

Contractions should be avoided. Spell out all words fully. Never write:

Can't	I've	Isn't	We've
Don't	Shouldn't	It'll	Won't

The ubiquitous "I"

I find I lose my patience when I read too many *I*'s, *my*'s, and *we*'s. A few are all right, but there is no excuse for half a dozen a page. Overuse of the vertical pronoun is a stylistic solecism only, but it should be avoided.

A problem might arise if you are directed to give your personal opinion on a subject. You might be inclined to commence in this fashion: "I recommend we buy the company. In arriving at my decision I examined costs, probable profits, and availability of capital. I did not feel it appropriate to consider legal implications as these are outside my area of control." Couldn't it be reworded as follows: "I recommend we buy the company. The decision was based on an examination of costs, probable profits, and availability of capital. Legal implications were not considered as these are outside my area of control."

Two *I*'s and a *my* have been eliminated with no weakening of the text. You will note the first *I* was not tampered with. The active *I recommend* is much stronger than the passive *It is recommended,* and the positive note struck by the *I* lets the reader know that the writer is taking full responsibility for his recommendation.

Careful editing should eliminate the personal pronoun problem.

I and we

An insurance company declines to issue a policy. Does the employee who relays this information to the client start his letter: "I regret I cannot . . ."? Does he write, "I regret we cannot . . ."? or does he phrase the decision this way: "We regret we cannot . . ."?

The English would call the quandary a sticky wicket and for good reason. When the writer uses two *I*'s as in the first example, he implies that he and he alone made the decision. He assumes full responsibility for the refusal. It is highly unlikely that a single individual, unless he holds a position of awesome authority, can unilaterally decide the issue on his own. He is probably guided by explicit company policy and in all likelihood has discussed the matter with a colleague or superior. Thus, to write, "I regret I cannot . . ." is neither candid nor totally accurate.

"I regret we cannot . . ." is much better. The *I* is a personal touch that might mitigate slightly the disappointment of the client on receiving the news. "We regret we cannot . . ." is colder, more impersonal.

All of us are familiar with the editorial *we*. We recall our amusement at the royal use of the pronoun by Queen Victoria when she said, "We are not amused." For those of us who are neither editorial writers nor empresses, the word *we* usually refers to the organization that pays our niggardly salaries while *I* refers to personal opinion. Thus: "I am concerned with the weakness in new car sales, and at General Motors we . . ."

Do not, by the use of *I,* assume authority not fully vested in you.

Is it all right to write: "I regret we cannot issue the policy, and I suggest that you . . ."? I think so. The company has turned down the client; you personally are sorry and suggest an alternative action. I find nothing wrong in that.

Consider for a moment the use of *I* and *we* in reports. "I recommend we commence construction of the new plant immediately." It is the writer's opinion that the company should build the plant. Executives are constantly being asked their personal opinions, decisions, and conclusions.

4

Replies should include the pronoun *I,* but when action ensues, the corporate *we* should be used.

Collective nouns

A company or a corporation is an *it,* not a *they.* A baseball team, though composed of nine members if we ignore the designated hitter which we and the game should do, is still an *it.* The theory behind this, I suppose, is that a company or a team is a group and as such is singular.

Few of us would use a plural verb when referring to a group. "The company *are* going to introduce a new product" sounds offensive to the ear as well as to our grammatical sense. But a goodly portion of us frequently err when we replace *The company* with a pronoun. We write or say, *"They* are going to . . ." instead of *"It* is going to . . ."

So far, so good, but here is where the waters become muddied. "The Steeler team leads the league." But, "The Steelers lead the league." Hardly news. In the first statement the verb is singular because the collective noun *team* is singular, and in the second the plural verb refers to the players on the team rather than to the organization itself.

In short, when the group or organization is referred to, a singular verb and pronoun should be used. When individuals that make up the group are discussed, plural forms should be used.

Redundant or unnecessary words

Never use several words when one will do the job. Why say *despite the fact that* when you can write *although* or *in the majority of cases* when *usually* means the same thing? Tenth graders, when assigned a theme of two hundred words, use

such circumlocutions to reach the desired number. Businessmen should have different objectives. Never use more words
than necessary to express your thought. Examples of wordy
expressions and their equivalents:

Aforesaid .... (Don't use at all)

As to whether .... Whether

At the present moment ..... Now

Due to .... Because

For the purpose of .... For

Hold a discussion .... Discuss

In depth analysis .... Analysis

In view of .... Because or since

In view of the fact that ..... (Even worse)

On a formal basis .... Formally

Should it transpire that ..... If

Take action .... Act

Take notice .... Notice or note

With respect to .... About, concerning

Another cause of redundancy is a lack of understanding
of the precise meaning of a word. Take *unique,* for example.
It means single, sole, without like. How then can anything
be *very* unique? *Consensus of opinion* is another clinker.
Consensus says it all on its own as it is defined as group soli-
darity in sentiment and belief.

Here are more expressions of the same ilk:

Deeply profound   Successfully convinced

Fellow colleague   Successful triumph

Fully competent   Surrounded on all sides

Important essential   Total ban

Occasional frequenter   Unexpected surprise

Technical subjects

A geologist writing a memo to others of similar training will use a technical vocabulary fully understandable to his peers. When he addresses a reader not familiar with the terms and expressions of his field, however, he would be wise to couch his statements in words understandable to intelligent people who have no specialized training in geology.

Marketeers talk to each other using terms such as *rollout, skimming, market segmentation, pull* and *push* promotions. Such terms might mystify the parent company's treasurer who was being asked for a substantial increase in the advertising budget.

Polysyllabic proliferation

The use of long, awkward, or unfamiliar words does not impress the reader with your erudition. On the contrary, he will be turned off if he feels you are deliberately trying to expose his illiteracy. Avoid verbal blockbusters. Keep it short and sweet.

Not long ago I came across a curious combination of letters in a piece of writing; "mneumatic." No such word exists, but the dictionary suggested the writer may have had one of these words in mind:

Pneumonic—Having to do with the lungs.

Pneumatic—Inner tube or buxom burlesque queen effect.

Mnemonic—Aid to memory—from Mnemosyne, Greek goddess of memory and mother, by Zeus, of the nine Muses. A fascinating character.

None of these words made much sense in the context of the writing, but during my research I happened upon the longest English word I have ever seen. It relegates antidisestablishmentarianism, a puny twenty-eight letters to the junior varsity.

Pneu-mo-no-ul-tra-mi-cro-scop-ic-sili-co-vol-ca-no-co-ni-o-sis. A lusty forty-five letters that describe a disease of the lungs caused by inhaling quartz dust. Which means more to you, the forty-five[1] letter word or the definition?

A more concise example of the wrong word in the right place is an excerpt from a recent news article describing the scene of a gang killing. "_____ was on the floor, the top of his head blown off and a cane-backed chair resting precipitously on his leg." How can an article at rest, in this instance a cane-backed chair, be described as *precipitous?* I wonder what the reporter was trying to say and what the rewrite man was dreaming when the story crossed his desk.

The moral to this is: don't use a combination of letters that cannot be found in a dictionary and don't use an unintelligible blockbuster when easily understood shorter substitutes are available.

Numbers

Eleven million, nine hundred sixteen thousand, five hundred thirty-seven dollars and sixteen cents. Fourteen words! Why not $11,916,537.16? Spelled out numbers take more space and are much more difficult to comprehend than numerals.

Yet, "The energy program will cost approximately $142,000,000,000." The eyes are boggled as well as the mind. When I see a number like that, I start at the right and say, "Hundreds, thousands, millions, billions," as I count each set of three zeros. Isn't *$142 billion* easier to read and equally effective?

A treasurer's report to his board will employ a number of figures. He will probably use numerals solely. Another report

[1] Numbers twenty-eight, forty-five, and forty-five have been spelled out as this is not a financial report containing many figures, and the numerals 28, 45, and 45 would appear to be out of place. See section on "Numbers."

may have only three numbers in it: 28, 45, 45. A better appearance might be achieved if the three simple figures were spelled out.

A savings bank will advertise 5½% interest on passbook accounts. To write *five and a half percent* would neither attract the eye or impress the mind. Either *10%* or *10 percent* is preferable to *double digit* in profane reference to inflation rates.

A rule of thumb followed by many newspapers is to spell out numbers through ten and use numerals from 11 up.

What have we decided about writing numbers? As I started to write this section, I thought I knew my . . . (No! Three *I*'s already and one *my*—rewrite.) I am convinced that . . . (No! Beware of phrases such as this.) Let us put it this way. There are no hard and fast rules covering writing numbers. Consider appearance and ease of comprehension, save as much space as possible, strive for clarity, and be as consistent as possible. Do not write *four* on one line and *5* on the next. Finally, whatever you do, do it for a reason—consider the alternatives first and adopt the best method of writing your numbers.

Having said there are no firm rules to cover number writing, I will now hedge. To start a sentence with numerals is definitely wrong. "1066 was the year of the Norman invasion." Either spell out *Ten sixty-six* or reword so the date appears later in the sentence. "The Norman invasion occurred in 1066."

Minor irritants

The word *prejudice* covers acres of ground. The dictionary says it means: "1. . . . . injury or damage resulting from some judgment or action of another in disregard of one's rights. . . . . 2. . . . . a preconceived judgment or opinion . . . . . (*c*) . . . . . an irrational attitude of hostility directed against an individual, a group, a race or their supposed characteristics....."[2] I deplore the curse of *prejudice* as presented in definitions 1 and *c* but rise in defense of *prejudice* as defined in 2. To me there is a basic heroic quality in being able to enjoy one's idiosyncratic hang-ups as long as they injure no one and affect only oneself. Consider that old epigram:

> I do not love thee, Doctor Fell;
> The reason why I cannot tell.
> But this I'm sure I know full well,
> I do not love thee, Doctor Fell.

The author, a certain T. Brown, is a man after my heart. The quatrain is a perfect example of number 2 *prejudice*, provided Dr. Fell was not a living person, or if he was, T. Brown kept his opinion to himself and did not broadcast it to the chagrin of Doctor Fell. The enjoyment of this type of sentiment is one of the pleasantest delights vouchsafed to man.

I used to receive in the interoffice mail a memo, the top of which looked like this:

· · · · · · · FROM THE DESK OF

W. G. RYCKMAN

My response, in the unlikely event there would be one, was always directed to the piece of furniture in question. Why it should be concerned with the matter in hand is a mystery, as is how it proposed to act on my reply. Since these missives irk me as much as they do, you might ask why I possess

---

[2] By permission. From *Webster's New Collegiate Dictionary* © 1979 by G. & C. Merriam Co., Publishers of the Merriam-Webster Dictionaries.

samples. Good question. Approximately seventeen years ago a printing salesman presented me with twenty pads of this form, each containing fifty sheets of paper. Every year since then I cut the top off a pad and use the clear section of the sheets as weekly reminders of things to be done. I have very few uncut sheets remaining.

Another type of number 2 *prejudice* is directed at people who advance an argument and then say, *as you can clearly see* . . . . Nobody tells me what I can clearly see. Perhaps my glasses are dirty or misplaced and I can't even see the end of my nose clearly. I may be asked to look, but I and I alone will determine what I can clearly see. Even that isn't right. It should be *see clearly,* not *clearly see.* The same goes for *it should be evident that . . . , I am sure you will agree that . . . ,* and similar effronteries.

One must be able to enjoy one's number 2 type *prejudices.* If one can't enjoy them, what is the point of nurturing them?

Let us return to the *From the Desk of* form for a moment. We must accept the conclusion that this is the *personalized* era. (Dear me, I have done it myself. I have no right to tell you what you should or should not accept. The sentence must be revised. "To me, the present is characterized as the *personalized* era." That's better even if the sentence does contain two *ized* words. My apologies.) We are surrounded on all sides (another slip—eliminate *on all sides,* or change to *beset on all sides,* please) by *personalized* towels, sheets, stationery, luggage, cuff links, pens and pencils, shirts, ad infinitum, ad nauseam. (Use of Latin phrases not generally recommended but perhaps acceptable in this questionable attempt at whimsical humor.) *Personalized* means only that one's name or initials appear on the article. Say that, if you must, but use of the word *personalized* is not to be tolerated. (My final solecism. Passive construction is weak; active is strong. Rephrase. ". . . but avoid the use of . . . .")

To find one's writing so poor is discouraging, especially

when one has the presumption to set himself up as an arbiter of writing style. This brief digression points out the insidious nature of the traps that await a writer. Maintain eternal vigilance. (Shouldn't I have said, "Be alert"? Why use three long pretentious words when two short snappy ones would do better?) Sharpened, blue, editing pencils are essential for writing vigorously, clearly, and concisely. (Note the three modifiers of *writing* and a like number for *pencils.* Use nouns and verbs—be sparing of adjectives and adverbs.)

As I write these words, my ear is tuned to the early morning radio news. Within the space of three minutes I have heard a former president, in an interview, say, ". . . to assure him *of the fact* that not only I but . . . ." I have heard an announcer declaim, in touting a product, "It is *very* unique, indeed." I have also heard a newscaster discussing the *scenario* of the falling Skylab. He considered the incident ". . . from the *people hazard* standpoint."

One is inclined to say, "Its spinach and to hell with it! If you can't beat em, join em." (Come, come, my friend. The contraction of *it is* is *it's. Them,* when contracted, becomes *'em.* Amen.)

More minor irritants

Irregardless. Never use. The word does appear in the dictionary but with the note, "nonstandard." Write *regardless* and save two letters.

Fact. "The Declaration of Independence was signed July 4, 1776." This is a fact. "Jimmy Carter is (was) a great president." Political implications aside, the statement is not a fact, because it relies on a personal valuation. This alone removes it from the *fact* category. There is a real distinction between facts and assumptions or conclusions. Don't mistake one for the other, and make your differentiation clear.

Different than. No. *Different from.*

Myriad. From the Greek, meaning: "1: Ten thousand; 2: an immense number." The second definition is the more widely used. "Myriad grains of sand on the beach." Never *a myriad of* anymore than one would refer to *a countless of* stars in the heavens.

Integrity of singular and plural. British writers perpetrate verbal rape on our language by switching from singular nouns to plural pronouns. Horrible. The practice has osmosed across the Atlantic. Eradicate it.

> "*Every man* should watch *their* step." *His.*
> The orchestra saved *their* best efforts for *their* final selection."
> *Its* twice.

A singular antecedent requires a singular pronoun.

Very. Use sparingly. A weak word; a useless adjective.

All right. There is no such word as *alright.*

Anybody. Usually one word. When written *any body,* it refers to one of several cadavers littering the premises.

Regionalisms. The subject embraces a number of heinous sins. I refer to this type of speech or writing as *hound dog.* Individuals on whom this opprobrious epithet is hung respond with rancor. Forget them!

> "Where is your car *at*?" Why not, "Where have you parked your car?" or even more simply, "Where is your car?"
>
> "I have no doubt *but* that . . . ." Say or write, "I have no doubt that . . ." or better yet, "I am sure that. . . ."
>
> "I *can't hardly* tell the difference." An unwitting double negative.

One regionalism is unavoidable. The English language has hundreds of thousands of words; I don't know how many. Yet, there is no way to describe the most common cause of a car coming to a stop on the highway. One person says, "I *ran* out of gas." Another laughs at this quaint expression and offers as replacement, "I *gave* out of gas." What can one say? I really do not know.

It is a strange language that we write and speak. "I woke up when the alarm clock went *off.*" In this sentence *off* means *on.*

I have been getting further and further away from regionalisms. You should do likewise.

Vague references and words. A writer rambles on for a page or two and then commences a new paragraph with: "This means that . . ." Quite properly the reader asks to what does *this* refer? *It* and *this* generally require an antecedent, something that clearly identifies what the *this* or *it* relates to.

Posture. Another in-word. We must adopt a posture for everything. Military *posture,* economic *posture,* foreign relations *posture.* As a callow youth I was constantly exhorted to improve my *posture.* My mother meant stand up straight, you round-shouldered, spaghetti-backed urchin. *Posture* does have another definition; frame of mind, attitude. Granted, but be sparing of use in this context.

7

Writing style and form

We have spent considerable time on the subject of words and it is now time to concern ourselves how to employ them to the greatest advantage. In doing so we will explore age-old fallacies relating to split infinitives and prepositions and touch on several types of what I call organizational punctuation: parentheses, brackets, slashes, and footnotes.

Finally we will get down to what this chapter is all about: writing style. Words are the tools of the writer's trade. The ones he picks and how he strings them together in sentences and paragraphs determines the quality of his style. There are as many different styles as there are writers and just as there are good writers and bad writers so are there good styles and bad styles. Remember your high school experiences with Addison and Steele, with Hazlitt and Lamb. I don't suppose any of us will attain the rare excellence in style reached by those essayists but at least we can be aware of some of the principles of good writing exemplified in their work. So, let's get right at it.

Split infinitives

To knowingly or unknowingly split an infinitive is not considered good grammatical form. Many people have no idea what an infinitive is and wouldn't know how to go about splitting one. Did you spot the glaring split in the first sentence?

Let us see how the dictionary defines an infinitive. It says it is: ".....a verb form normally identical in English with the first person singular that performs some functions of a noun and at the same time displays some characteristics of a verb and that is used with *to* ..... except with auxiliary and various other verbs....."[1] Forget it! Our lexicographer is turning into a waffler spouting bureaucratese. Also note his disgusting double use of that meaningless vague modifier *some*.

For our purpose an infinitive is a verb preceded by the word *to*. Thus: "To curse fluently is an art." *To curse* is our infinitive, and to split it all we have to do is move *fluently* between the two parts of the infinitive. "To fluently curse is an art" contains our split infinitive. What law have we broken and why is it such a dastardly crime? I haven't the foggiest except Miss Weller, in the sixth grade, told me I must never, never, split an infinitive. I haven't done it since.

Actually, "To curse fluently..." sounds better than "To fluently curse...." The ear should be the final arbiter. "I can't force myself to actually root for the Yankees." That sounds normal; my ear is not offended, although denizens of the Bronx may not agree with my sentiments. To say, "I can't force myself actually to root for the Yankees," sounds awkward, stilted.

When you split an infinitive, be aware of what you are doing. Split it only if your ear tells you that you should. Would a complete change of sentence structure suit your purpose even better? Be your own judge, but what you do, do deliberately.

[1] By permission. From Webster's New Collegiate Dictionary © 1979 by G. & C. Merriam Co., Publishers of the Merriam-Webster Dictionaries.

Ending a sentence with a preposition

A preposition is the part of speech used to relate a noun to another word in a sentence.

"He knocked *on* the door." *On* is the preposition that relates *door,* a noun, with the verb *knocked.*

Among the most common prepositions are:

At	Of
Before	Off
By	On
For	To
From	Up
In	With

One of the first rules of grammar I learned was that a preposition should never be used to end a sentence. Why not? No one ever told me because I suspect there is no valid reason not to. (Not bad.) There is, I agree, something unattractive about a well-rounded sentence ending abruptly with an *of,* a *to,* a *for,* or a *with.* Yet, change in construction may result in even more undesirable results.

"What are we waiting for?" Would you prefer, "For what are we waiting?" I wouldn't.

But, "There are the feathers you should stuff the pillow with." No. "Stuff the pillow with those feathers." Preferable, provided one is not allergic to feathers.

"What were you thinking of?" sounds better than "Of what were you thinking?" Doesn't it?

It all depends on the ear. (Come now, what does the *it* refer to? Come again. Shouldn't I have written, "To what does *it* refer?" No way.)

Confused? Don't be. Know what you are doing, but let your judgment and your ear control what you do.

Active and passive voices

Whenever possible, avoid the passive voice; it is weak, stilted, and usually leaves questions in the mind of the reader.

"It is expected that mortgage rates will continue to rise over the next quarter."

Who expects rates to rise? Why should the reader believe such a statement? "I expect mortgage rates to rise over the next quarter because . . . ." Now the reader has information on which to base his acceptance or rejection of the statement. Perhaps the writer of the first sentence was trying to avoid the use of the personal pronoun. Good for him, but in this instance the weakness of the statement is more unacceptable than the use of *I*.

Suffixes -ize, -wise, -ship

"We must prioritize our inputs economywise." The writer possibly means we should establish an order of importance in considering steps to effect savings. At least he did not tell us that *prioritization* is essential.

To many misguided people, adding *-ize* or *-wise* to a word sounds highly professional. We *finalize, maximize, strategize.* One of the first women ordained by the Episcopal Church said: "I will not let the church inferiorize me again." Bully for her. She certainly achieved self-actualization personality-wise.

In 1940 German Panzers swept through France and the Lowlands. Today a correspondant might report: "Situation-wise, inputs from France indicate maximized nonsuccess battlewise." Churchill said: "The news from France is bad."

Ize and *wise* don't add. They detract from clear forceful writing. Avoid them.

Ship is another overused and misused suffix. This morning I actually heard a radio announcer say: "Amelioration of the gas shortage has impacted in a negative manner on Metro ridership." She used the word *ridership* twice more in the next twenty seconds. (No, I am not unaware of the misuse of *impacted.*)

Each usage bothered me because the word sounded contrived, artificial. I felt very virtuous until I suddenly recalled Miss Weller, who, more than half a century ago, strove valiantly but unsuccessfully to teach me *penmanship.* A horrible word but how about *penwomanship?*

Footnotes

In general, business memos and reports are not similar to academic or scientific papers in which every statement must be supported by a specific reference to its direct source. Footnotes are distracting to a businessman. They disturb the flow of his reading, especially if they are accumulated at the end of the report and he is forced to go back and forth to refer to them. Avoid them whenever possible.

Some highly technical reports will require footnotes, and they should appear at the bottom of the page below a line that clearly indicates they are not part of the text.[2]

Parentheses and brackets

In nearly every situation commas can be used in place of parentheses. Stay with the familiar and avoid the unfamiliar punctuation symbols. "The increase of Accounts Receivable (if it continues at the present rate) will have a serious . . . ." Here commas are preferable to parentheses.

Parentheses may be used when referring to exhibits. "Costs are estimated at $450,000. (See Exhibit III.)"

Normally it is not necessary to include numerals in paren-

---

[2] If you must have footnotes, use this form.

theses to emphasize a written number. "There are now fifty (50) stars in our flag." Flush the *(50)*.

Brackets are used to enclose extraneous matter in a quotation. "*Almayer's Folly* [Conrad's first novel] was published in 1895." They are also used to enclose the Latin word *sic* when you wish to draw attention to an error in a quotation. "The dog was chasing it's [sic] tail." Whenever I am confronted by this usage of brackets, I get the impression the writer arrogantly assumes I am too ignorant to spot the mistake. A murrain on him.

Equal rights in gender, leading to a discussion of the slash

Chairman, Chairwoman, Chairperson
Mrs., Miss, Ms.
A person is entitled to his/her opinion.

Who in his/her right mind voluntarily chooses a perch between Ossa and Pelion? What man/woman steers his/her craft deliberately between Scylla and Charybdis?

Make up your own mind and do whatever you please, but include me out of the battle.

Another digression rears its ugly head. You will note the use of the slash (/) in preceding paragraphs. There, the punctuation mark was used to indicate an option. It is also employed to indicate the end of a line of poetry incorporated in the text. "The first version of Blake's 'The Tyger' commences 'Tyger, tyger, burning bright/ In the forests of the night.'"

The most common use of the slash is in *and/or*. This is pure legalese. Don't use it. "Production and/or marketing are (is?) involved in the problem." The writer means that the problem involves either production or marketing or perhaps both divisions. Let him say so.

The slash is acceptable when used to designate a unit composed of several separate entities. For instance: "Sales can be expanded in Parkersburg, Wheeling or in Morgantown/ Fairmont/Clarksburg." The first two cities named are separate territories. The combined area around the last three cities named would be considered as a single territory. In this example, use of the slash saves space and is readily understandable.

Overkill in writing

In a written business communication reiteration is redundancy. Write it once, write it clearly, and then go on to the next point. Don't repeat yourself. There is a hoary old saw (mind how you spell hoary) to the effect that when making a speech, one tells the audience what one is going to say, then says it, and concludes by telling the audience what it has been told. This is fine for some speeches but unacceptable in a relatively short written report.

The written word endures forever. Once a statement is made, it need never be repeated. There is no place in a report for such phrases as "to recapitulate what I have previously stated" or "as I mentioned earlier." Say it once, say it firmly, concisely, and clearly.

To add a touch of inconsistency, in a lengthy report some concession to this precept may be necessary, but needless repetition should be avoided.

The observant reader of this section will discover that I have made a simple statement: *don't repeat yourself,* and then said the same thing in slightly different words at least six more times. How's that for consistency?

Rhetorical questions

Don't ask a question unless you are prepared to handle the response. I once was a member of an organization of friendly souls who/that[3] held an annual banquet at which the new slate of officers was installed. Before and during dinner spirits ran high. When the retiring president rose to introduce his successor, he planned to offer a glowing tribute to the new leader. He started with a rhetorical question, "Who is Meredith and what has he done for us?"[4] That was as far as he got. There was a wild uproar in the audience. Shouts of "Who the hell cares," "Not a damn thing," could be heard.

The sterling character and outstanding achievements of our new president remained a deep secret. A year later Meredith did not open his speech with a rhetorical question.

In writing also, rhetorical questions are to be avoided. Don't ask a question and then answer it. That approach is a time and space waster, and it irritates the reader.

"I examined the financial situation and what did I find?" Awful. Examine the situation and tell us what you found.

"What, you may ask, will be the consequences of this law?" Rubbish. "The consequences of this law will be . . . ."

Dogmatic statements

Beware of overuse of such phrases as:

I believe
I think
I feel
It is my opinion

Especially beware of:

I am certain
I am positive

---

[3] *Who* if referring to souls, *that* if referring to organization. Unclear. Rewrite.
[4] Ben Jonson got away with it when he wrote: "Who is Sylvia? What is she?"

To be avoided at all costs:

> I am absolutely convinced

If such phrases are followed by one or more "becauses," the writer should say, "I conclude" rather than, "I think." A reasoned conclusion has more weight than an unsupported statement.

Never does vehemence of language make up for faulty logic. Readers are suspicious when a writer attempts to steamroller them into agreement.

Don't be dogmatic in your Olympian pronouncements:

> Everyone knows . . .
>
> There can be no argument with the conclusion that . . .
>
> It is an accepted fact . . .
>
> Clearly . . .

Such statements irritate a reader and give him an opportunity to display his perverse streak. What might be crystal clear to you might not be as apparent to him. Convince him with the weight of your logic and allow him to decide if the purported fact is indeed acceptable to him.

Sentence structure

What is a sentence? (Is it *alright* [sic] for me to start this section with a rhetorical question or should I have begun, "A sentence is . . ."?) The dictionary has a number of definitions for *sentence,* only two of which are relevant. The first starts this way: ". . . . . A grammatically self-contained speech unit consisting of a word or a syntactically related group of words that expresses an assertion, a question, a command, a wish, or an exclamation, that in writing usu. begins with a capital letter and concludes with appropriate end punctuation, and that in speaking is phonetically distinguished by various patterns of stress, pitch, and pauses.....".[5] How does that grab you? The other definition of the word used as a verb is: "to cause to suffer something." Definition number two perfectly describes the result of trying to understand definition number one.

If that is what a sentence is, who can bewail the inability of writers to compose a simple declarative sentence? It must be harder than it looks.

Yet, we have only scratched the surface. There are simple sentences, complex sentences, compound sentences, compound-complex sentences, run-on sentences, loose sentences, balanced sentences: their name is legion.

I have no intention of making this section a treatise on grammar. I am not competent to do so and leave the field to properly trained eighth-grade English teachers who have the most difficult and frustrating job in the world.

Let us dally for a moment, however, on the subject of sentences.

"Run!" That is a sentence according to the definition. It is one word, expresses a complete thought in the form of a command, begins with a capital letter and has appropriate end punctuation.

"The man runs." Here we have a subject and verb.

"The tall man runs slowly." Both subject and verb have a modifier. The adjective *tall* precedes the noun *man* while the adverb *slowly* follows the verb *runs.*

"The tall young man, clad in a jogging outfit, runs slowly along the path." Somewhat more complex but perfectly clear.

"The tall young man, clad in a dirty blue jogging outfit

[5] By permission. From Webster's New Collegiate Dictionary © 1979 by G. & C. Meriam Co., Publishers of the Merriam-Webster Dictionaries.

with green stripes, runs slowly along the rutted dirt path that winds through the beeches, oaks, and aspens of Birnam Wood." That's about as much mileage as we can expect to get out of this sentence. Any more descriptive information crammed into it would result only in confusion.

How about word order? We could have said, "Slowly, the tall man runs." The emphasis is now on *slowly*. In similar fashion we could rearrange the next sentence to read: "Clad in a jogging outfit, the tall man runs along the path slowly." Emphasis again is changed, but I don't like the position of *slowly*. It is too close to *path* and too far from *runs,* the verb it modifies.

If we alter the order of the final sentence, total confusion results and meaning is obscured. All examples are *simple* sentences, containing no dependent clauses; even so the final one is complex enough for an ordinary reader.

What does all this prove? How long or how short should a sentence be? What should be the word order? A writer should strive for variety of structure, but clarity is the primary objective. Variety is necessary so the mind and eye will not be bored by the monotony of sentence after sentence of the same length and construction. Writing style and custom have changed over the years. A study disclosed that three hundred years ago written sentences averaged about sixty words; a hundred years ago the average had fallen to about thirty. Subject matter affects sentence length. An instruction manual accompanying a "Make-It-Yourself Atom Bomb Kit" that employed sixty-word sentences to explain highly technical details of construction might trigger a premature explosion.

In 1767 Laurence Sterne wrote *A Sentimental Journey.* The reverend doctor's concept of punctuation is not as modern as his approach to what we now call situational ethics; so I shall start the excerpt with the words that follow the last period that appears in the work. To set the scene: Sterne stopped at a small inn and engaged the only bedroom which, by chance, contained two beds. In the evening, a Piedmontese lady of about thirty "with a glow of health on her cheek," accompanied by a "brisk and lively" maid of twenty, also stopped at the inn. Sterne politely offered the other bed to the lady, and a formal agreement was reached regarding the decorum of the two principals during the enforced sharing of the chamber. The sleepless Sterne, in the middle of the night, broke Article 3 of the agreement by ejaculating, "Oh, my God." The lady, apparently also suffering from insomnia, immediately charged him with a treaty violation. Now—to our sentence.

> Upon my word and honor, Madame, said I—stretching my arms out of bed by way of asservation—
> —(I was going to have added, that I would not have trespass'd against the remotest idea of decorum for the world)—
> —But the Fille de Chambre hearing there were words between us, and fearing that hostilities would ensue in course, had crept silently out of her closet, and it being totally dark, had stolen so close to our beds, that she had got herself into the narrow passage which separated them and had advanced so far up as to be in a line between her mistress and me—
> So that when I stretched out my hand, I caught hold of the Fille de Chambre's—
>
> THE END OF THE SECOND VOLUME

One is scarcely aware that the sentence does not conclude with an appropriate end punctuation.

Let us now leap ahead to 1899 when Conrad wrote *Lord Jim.* An explanation of the situation is not necessary for understanding of this excerpt from the climax of the novel.

> Jim came up slowly, looked at his dead friend, lifting the sheet, then dropped it without a word. Slowly he walked back.

"He came! He came!" was running from lip to lip, making a murmur to which he moved. "He hath taken it upon his own head," a voice said aloud. He heard this and turned to the crowd. "Yes, Upon my head." A few people recoiled. Jim waited awhile before Doramin, and then said gently, "I am come in sorrow." He waited again. "I am come ready and unarmed," he repeated.

Great writing by two masters of prose—I hope you will agree—but poles apart in many ways. Each author captures the mood for which he strives; each word has a purpose; each concept is clear. Writing like this doesn't just happen; it doesn't spring fully formed from the brain of the author.

Hemingway may unconsciously have emulated Conrad; Faulkner is more akin to Sterne in structure if not imagery. What happens to sentences when one is neither a Sterne, a Conrad, a Hemingway, nor a Faulkner?

Let us start by correcting an obvious fault. "He saw a rainbow going downtown." Rewrite. "As he was going downtown, he saw a rainbow." Eliminate the dangling participle.

"Shooting par frequently is a golfer's ambition." Does *frequently* refer to *shooting par* or *ambition?* How you write it depends on what you mean. Be sure what your modifier modifies.

"The point at which you order being your order point which is a combination of your requirements during lead time plus a buffer stock which will cover us in case of any undue fluctuations in demand."

That collection of words starts with a capital letter and ends with a period, but that doesn't make it a sentence. After two or three readings one realizes what the writer is trying to say. The trouble is he started babbling and never took himself sternly in hand. What he is attempting to tell us is that stock should be reordered far enough in advance to allow for normal use during the time between the order and the expected delivery of the order. He states also that a cushion to cover unexpected high demand in the interval should be maintained. How would you express these thoughts clearly and succinctly to your purchasing department?

If you can handle that one, try this: "Further, unless petroleum prices do not become prohibitive (which is unlikely since petroleum is not a renewable resource) plastics may not continue to make significant inroads into paper products." Here our fledgling Homer had no clear concept of what he wanted to say when he picked up his pen. He started with a vague idea and plowed ahead without ever considering where his rhetoric or his syntax was taking him.

Clarify your thoughts before you start to write and hope you will never involve yourself in a quadruple negative that defies translation into understandable prose.

Here is another gem that on the surface appears fairly easy to correct.

"The fact that all the aforementioned management owns at least some stock in the company should make for their commitment to making it a success greater than otherwise."

Prolix, convoluted, ungrammatical. Will this do? "Since all management owns stock in the company, it will work harder for its success." Simpler—certainly—but still not absolutely clear. In the original, *management,* a singular noun is properly given a singular verb *owns.* Later the writer uses *their,* a plural pronoun referring to *management.* In the revision the correct *it* is used, but this *it* is confused by the *its* referring to *company.* So: "All management, owning stock in the company, will work harder for the company's success." If we feel we should emphasize the ownership factor more heavily, we might write: "Since all management owns stock in the company, each manager will work harder for the company's success." That is probably the concept the writer wanted to get across to the reader.

Is it necessary to take a microscope to every sentence we write? I should hope not, but sentences must be examined carefully if we are to be precise in our meaning, if we are to be clearly understood. A ray of hope: if you know what point you are going to make before you start a sentence, you have a better chance of expressing it clearly.

Professional status in constructing sentences that are totally unintelligible is reserved for bureaucrats who have spent years learning the art of obfuscation. What normal mortal could coin this sentence contained in a HUD report?

"Action-oriented orchestration of innovative inputs, generated by escalation of meaningful indiginous decision-making dialogue, focusing on multi-linked problem complexes, can maximize the vital thrust toward a non-alienated and viable urban infrastructure." Pure genius!

Stick with nouns and verbs. Use adjectives and adverbs sparingly. Do not string nouns together in a stately array. Do not run sentences on interminably, covering a half-dozen different subjects. Use a normal, standard English vocabulary.

Paragraphs

The dictionary defines a paragraph as: "..... a subdivision of a written composition that consists of one or more sentences, deals with one point or gives the words of one speaker, and begins on a new, usu. indented line....."[6] (Dear me, does *that* refer to *subdivision* or *composition?* Unclear. Rewrite.)

Please note that a paragraph *deals with one point.* It would be entirely proper to cover the creation of the earth in a single paragraph. It would not be proper in one paragraph to describe in detail the specific acts performed on each of the

---

[6] Ibid.

six days it took to do the job. Each day should be assigned its own paragraph.

Excessively long paragraphs intimidate a reader. No executive cares to look at a page-long, solid block of print in a report. Break it up; reassure the brain of the reader that it will not be overtaxed merely by wading through the prose. Don't try to cover too much in a paragraph; remember the *one-point* rule. Give marketing a paragraph, allocate another to production and still another to finance. Don't cram everything into a single compact mass.

In grammar school we learned that a paragraph should have a topic sentence—one that prepares the reader for what follows. There should also be a smooth transition from one paragraph to the next so there will be a flow of language and thought from one to the other—no abrupt change in direction, no surprises.

Successful writers of business reports use headings for the various sections of their papers. These headings, like the ones we have employed throughout this book, are great word savers. They replace the topic sentence that otherwise would be required. The writer, having said what was required in the section on Marketing, drops down two spaces and writes:

<u>Production</u>

The reader knows exactly what is coming next, and the writer can plunge into what he wants to say. It is not necessary for him to state in his final sentence on marketing that, having completed his analysis of that subject, he will now direct his attention to production.

Underlined headings serve another important purpose. They make it easy for a reader to locate a section of the report he wishes to reread, which is a great help when the report is a long one.

Internal policy in some corporations does not approve

indentation of the first line of a paragraph. My preference is in favor of indentation—it does break up the monotony of a page. Also, I see no reason to double-space between paragraphs as long as they are addressing the same primary subject.

When the section on Marketing is complete, however, I do suggest dropping down two lines before writing the new heading.

Headings should be underlined using a single continuous line rather than underlining one word at a time.

<u>Energy Requirements for the Next Decade</u>   Yes

<u>Energy Requirements for the Next Decade</u>   No

Broken lines make for slow reading and poor appearance.

Use upper and lower case when writing headings, reserving all capitals for emergencies:

<u>IMMINENT BANKRUPTCY</u>

Reference books

Two books should always be within reach of a writer: a dictionary and a thesaurus.

Use the dictionary to check your spelling and the meaning of words. Use it also as a guide to pronunciation should you fear you might have to read aloud what you have written. Few people realize the wealth of miscellaneous information contained in dictionaries.

You will find rules for spelling, for forming plurals and compounds, and for punctuation, capitalization, and italicization (quite a word). You will be instructed how to address a member of the Catholic brotherhood; you will note that the ZIP code of Cedar Crest College in Allentown, Pennsylvania, is 18104; and you will learn that Godwin Austen, also called

K2, is, at 28,250 feet, the second highest peak in the world. You will also be made aware that Howrah is a city on the Hooghly River opposite Calcutta and boasts a population of almost 600,000 inhabitants.

Believe it or not, dictionaries can be fun.

A thesaurus is quite another matter. Be sure your copy is printed in dictionary form. Originally, thesauri were arranged in sections, and a word with several meanings—such as *green*— would appear in a number of different categories. As a result, a voluminous index would have to be consulted before the proper section could be located. In the *Dictionary Form* the various meanings are collected in a single listing, and synonyms are shown for each meaning. Thus, we are told that the color *green* may be described as emerald, chartreuse, jade, olive, to name a few tints and shades, and that *green* also means callow, raw, inexperienced, or youthful. In the same listing we find *green* means lawn, terrace, grass. Normally, noun, adjective, verb, and adverb forms are given.

Often one needs a synonym to eliminate the necessity to repeat the same word over and over again in a written work. An *expenditure* can be an *expense,* a *disbursement,* an *outlay,* a *waste.* At times one seeks shading in a word to express precise thought. Is a *thief* an *embezzler,* a *safecracker,* a *bandit,* a *robber,* a *swindler?* The thesaurus will suggest the right word.

In addition, the book is essential for a rapid (speedy, expeditious, quick, fast, alacritous) solution of the Sunday *Times* double acrostic.

Misguided high school teachers of English have been known to recommend the use of a thesaurus to students so they can use sesquipedalian (a foot-and-a-half-long) words in their themes instead of better short ones. Teachers like that should be decollated instanter (beheaded at once). Use the thesaurus, but use it for the proper purpose.

8

Editing

I am reluctant to discuss this subject as I fear it will prove to be a difficult assignment. Yet, editing is such an integral part of writing it cannot be ignored. Few mortals can write fluent, grammatical, forceful prose off the tops of their heads. There is a room in the British Museum where manuscripts of famous authors are displayed. A page in the handwriting of Anthony Trollope, a benign and civilized Victorian novelist, indicates he was one of the lucky few. His first draft was his finished work. Trollope was unique in that he worked not like an artist but as an artisan, assigning himself regular hours at his desk and a fixed number of pages of manuscript to be produced, depending on the press of work in his regular job and whether he had to meet a publisher's deadline. On the average he assigned himself about forty pages a week. He tells us: "And as a page is an ambiguous term, my page has been made to contain 250 words; and as words, if not watched, will have a tendency to straggle, I have had every word counted as I went." Think of that; 10,000 finished words a week, and don't forget he turned out as many as 112 pages when the need arose.

Well, as far as I could tell, there were about 250 words on the page I scrutinized and not one correction or revision marred the sheet. A page of Lewis Carroll's *Alice in Wonderland* is equally uncluttered with changes. Not so with James Joyce. He crosses out, adds, revises, adds again, deletes, changes to the point that the page is indecipherable. I am not convinced the typesetter set what he was supposed to set or that Joyce knew the difference. The revision was no more intelligible to me than the original draft had been.

One can spend a fascinating hour or two in the museum observing the workings of genius. I apologize. This digression has been rather lengthy, the purpose of which is to impress on you, gentle reader, that some few crumbs of culture have dribbled onto my waistcoat. Another reason, perhaps, is that I don't quite know how to begin a section on editing.

This time the dictionary is of little assistance. It mumbles about editing the complete works of an author, editing out or deleting and that's about it. Mr. Webster is probably in the same boat with me. I'll have to take a chance and do it on my own. Editing, to me, consists of ensuring that:

1. Words are spelled correctly.
2. The right words are used to express precise meaning.
3. Sentences are grammatically and syntactically correct.
4. Punctuation follows accepted standards.
5. Paragraphs are of manageable length and observe the *one-point* principle.
6. The whole work is cohesive, flows logically step to step.

Following those directions is predominantly a mechanical task. Liken yourself to an artist creating a mosaic out of small, odd-shaped bits of colored stone. It is not enough to fit the pieces neatly together and cement them securely to the base. Any competent artisan could do that. The artistic test is whether the assembled bits form a picture that tells the story the artist has in mind. It is also essential that the artist have a story that has meaning for his audience. Artists deal in stone, paints, ceramics—any medium that meets their taste. Writers have only words at their disposal, and the quality of their work depends entirely on how they use their material. So, the editor's next task is to attend to these points:

1. Have unnecessary words been eliminated?
2. Are all thoughts clearly expressed and easily understood?
3. What about vague adjectives, too many adverbs?
4. Has gobbledygook been eliminated? What about business-ese, clichés, slang, coarseness?
5. Is the writing stiff and stilted or too casual and folksy?
6. Is the writer's attitude friendly, courteous?

Once he has made necessary improvements, our editor is ready for his most important task. He rereads the entire work with four thoughts in mind:

1. Has the reader been given all the information he needs?
2. Has he been given answers to questions he might ask?
3. Has the report fulfilled the assignment?
4. Does the report read as if it has been written by a human being? (Frequently this is not the case.)

It is extremely helpful if the writer can put himself in the place of the reader and look at the work through that person's eyes. Knowing the idiosyncracies of the reader is important; does he demand details, does he want to know the source of every bit of information contained in the report? What are his likes and dislikes? Cater to his wishes; put him in a receptive frame of mind. He may be a bull, but you don't have to wave your red flannels at him.

The writer turned editor, when he reads his work for the last time, should study the words he has written and ignore whatever else was in his mind when he wrote them. The reader has no crystal ball; he knows only what he sees. You may know what you meant when you made a statement. The test is whether the words you wrote express your meaning accurately. Failure to meet this test is a principal cause of weakness in written reports.

That's about the best I can do on editing. To sum it up, I would suggest that when a writer turns himself into an editor of his own work, he should split himself into several individuals: his grammar school English teacher, his reader, a pragmatic businessman who can analyze the written word, and a person sensitive to the impression the attitude of the writer will have on the reader.

An exercise in editing

An objective study of rules and principles is one thing; putting to work what one has learned is quite another, and the time has come for us to revise, correct, and edit the president's message in the annual report of Pin-Up Corporation.

This report is our introduction to a unique company, its colorful president and chief executive officer, Pevley Clip, and his brilliant young assistant, Charley Lightfoot, a Princeton educated descendant of famed Cherokee chieftains. Pin-Up, with headquarters in Shelbyville, Tennessee, is the largest manufacturer of clothespins in the south-central section of the state and has purveyed its wares successfully throughout the country for more than a hundred years. Pevley and his family own a controlling interest in the company, but the remainder of the stock is held by approximately two hundred individuals, and the president feels they are entitled to receive annually a complete and attractively printed report covering company operations. For several years Charley has written the message for his boss.

As soon as the books are closed, Charley gets a full set of financial statements from the comptroller, Eishade Waterhouse, and studies them carefully. He has already made himself familiar with other factors that have affected the results for the year just ended.

Charley knows Clip wants a short, snappy report. It must be straightforward but contain no explicit plans for the future since copies of the report will find their way to the hands of the competition, and Pevley is the last man in the world to give aid and comfort to the enemy.

Here is Charley's first draft:

> To All Stockholders:
>
> It is with the greatest pleasure that I report the 1979 results to you. For the seventeenth consecutive year your company has set new sales and profit records. Additionally, dividends were increased for the fifteenth straight year. Our plants are running at near capacity, and despite usual strong competition, our distribution channels are holding and in many areas increasing our share of the market.
>
> During the year just completed, we introduced two new products. The first, a giant-size pin for the use in areas where strong winds prevail, is selling better than projected in the Virginias, Tennessee, North Carolina, and the Rocky Mountain states. Results are disappointing in New England where the necessary price increase has inhibited sales. Market strategies in that area are being revalued.
>
> The second innovation, a wooden pin with strong wire spring, is doing well in test areas, and we will effect a rollout to the entire East in the next six months.
>
> The market for special orders remains firm, and this profitable sideline will continue to be exploited to the fullest extent possible.
>
> Financially your company is stronger than ever. Current ratio is better than 2.4 to 1, and although short-term notes payable have increased substantially in order to finance a much needed inventory increase, it is expected that they will be all paid off on or before June 30 of the current year.
>
> One of the greatest strengths of your company is the high morale of the many loyal employees in our plants and offices throughout the country. More innovations will be marketed this year, and we are confident in projecting even improved performance in 1980.
>
> I offer my thanks to you for your continued support.
>
> Pevley Clip
> President

Charley studies what he has written, and the longer he looks at it, the less he likes it. This experience is not new; so, undaunted, he picks up his blue pencil and goes to work. The next two right-hand pages contain the notes Charley made when he reread the first draft, and the left-hand pages show what the message looked like after revisions and corrections.

To All Stockholders:

The year 1979 was an excellent one
~~It is with the greatest pleasure that I report~~
for your company. Sales and profits rose again
~~1979 results to you. For the seventeenth consecutive year~~
as they have every year since 1963.
~~your company has set new sales and profit records.~~ ~~Additionally,~~
                                                                      at present
Dividends were increased for the fifteenth straight year. ∧ Our
                          close to   *sales,*
plants are running ~~at near~~ capacity and ∧ despite ~~usual strong~~
                   continue strong.
competition, ∧ ~~our distribution channels are holding and in~~

~~many areas increasing our share of the market.~~

During the year ~~just completed~~ we introduced ~~two~~

~~new products. The first,~~ a giant•size pin for use in areas
          heavy   *Sales are exceeding expectations*
where ~~strong~~ winds prevail, ~~is selling better than projected~~
in all but one area.
~~in the Virginias, Tennessee, North Carolina and the Rocky~~

~~Mountain states. Sales are disappointing in New England~~

~~where the necessary price increase has inhibited sales.~~

~~Market strategies in that area are being reevalued.~~

← ~~The second innovation,~~ A wooden pin with a strong
          sold so   *that over* ←
wire spring ∧ ~~is doing~~ well in test areas ~~and~~ we will ~~effect~~
market it in   *on part of the country.*
~~a roll out to~~ the entire east ∧ ~~in~~ (the next six months.)

~~The market for~~ Special orders ~~remains firm and~~
          are
~~this~~ ∧ profitable ~~side-line will continue to be exploited to~~

~~the fullest extent possible~~ *and we will continue*
our efforts to expand this segment of our
business.

¶ 1.   Flowery. Not like Mr. Clips. Change. _Seventeenth_ and _fifteenth_ too much. Awkward — eliminate one. Change _at near_ to _close to_. Delete unnecessary _usual_, _strong_. Distribution channels don't _hold_ or _increase_ anything. Rewrite. _Share of market_ — too technical. Restructure whole ¶.

¶ 2 + 3.   Compress to single ¶. First sentence wordy — rewrite. Flesh _geography_ — rewrite _New England_. Why allude to failure there? Flesh unnecessary words. _Strong_ used twice — change. Change _roll-out_. Rewrite whole sentence.

¶ 4.   If special orders are profitable they aren't a _sideline_. Rewrite _exploited..._ _fullest extent possible_. Stilted — eliminate.

Financially your company is stronger than ever. ~~Current ratio is better than 2.4 to 1, and although~~ Short-term notes payable have increased substantially in order to finance a much needed inventory increase, ~~it is~~ but we expected ~~that~~ they will be ~~all~~ paid off by the middle of the ~~on or before June 30 of the~~ current year.

One of the greatest strengths of your company is the high morale of the ~~many loyal~~ employees in our plants and offices throughout the country. To a large extent ~~More innovations will~~ our success can be attributed to their loyalty ~~be marketed this year and we are confident in projecting~~ and dedication to their responsibilities. ~~even improved performance in 1980.~~

~~I offer my~~ Thanks ~~to~~ you for your continued support.

Pevley Clip
President

Our financial condition is excellent; so is our competitive position. New products have been developed and will be introduced this year. Although the national economy appears to be in a recession with no firm indication of a quick recovery and although inflation poses a continuing threat to real prosperity, nevertheless, we are confident that at the end of this year we will again be able to report record sales and earnings.

P 5. First sentence OK — cheers!
How many stockholders recognize a
current ratio? Those that are
interested will work out the figure
from the balance sheet that appears
in the report. It is expected — weak — Flush.
Eliminate unnecessary words.

P 6. Violates one point principle. Keep up
compliment to employees.

P 7. Add. Beat the drums. Get a new
closing. I know we can do even better
this year. Mr. Clip is positive we
will. So, let's stick out our necks for
1980. At some time acknowledge
unfavorable economic conditions.
Close — stilted — reword.

Charley realizes no one in his office could decipher his hieroglyphics; so he dusts off his trusty Underwood and laboriously types out a clear copy of the revised message. It looks like this:

To All Stockholders:

The year 1979 was an excellent one for your company. Sales and profits rose again as they have every year since 1963. Dividends were increased for the fifteenth straight year. At present, plants are running close to capacity, and sales, despite competition, continue strong.

During the year we introduced a giant-size pin for use in areas where heavy winds prevail. Sales are exceeding expectations in all but one locality. A wooden pin with a strong wire spring sold so well in test areas that over the next six months we will market it in the entire eastern part of the country.

Special orders are profitable, and we will continue our efforts to expand this segment of our business.

Financially your company is stronger than ever. Short-term notes payable have increased substantially in order to finance a much needed inventory increase, but we expect they will be paid off by the middle of the current year.

One of the greatest strengths of our company is the high morale of the employees in our plants and offices throughout the country. To a large extent our success can be attributed to their loyalty and dedication to responsibilities.

Our financial condition is excellent, so is our competitive position. New products have been developed and will be introduced this year. Although the national economy appears to be in a recession with no firm indication of a quick recovery and although inflation poses a continuing threat to real prosperity, nevertheless, we are confident that at the end of this year we will again be able to report record sales and earnings.

Thank you for your continued support.

Pevley Clip
President

Charley likes the way the message reads—concise, smooth, and it sounds as if the old man had written it himself. He makes a copy for his file, sends the original to the boss, and decides there is time for a cup of coffee and a stroll through the plant before he tackles his next assignment. All is well with Charley and Pin-Up.

9
Letter writing

How's this for starters?

> Dere sir
>
>   Inclosed is $4 Plese
> send ~~yu~~ yore book
> beter riting to Sam'l Johnsom.
>   R F D 1
>   Frog Hollow
>   W. Va 89706
>
>   Singed
>   Sam'l Johnson

I have been spending an unconscionable amount of time reading what the competition has to say about letter writing. All the experts talk about starting with a good quality white paper measuring 8½ by 11 inches, go on through heading, inside address, salutation, body, complimentary (whatever that connotes) close, and signature. Strangely enough, not one mentions that every letter should be dated. The reader is told what size envelope he should use, how to fold the sheet of good quality white paper, and that a stamp of the proper denomination should be affixed to the upper right-hand corner of the envelope or the mailman won't deliver the letter. A number of experts mention Block or Modified Block style. I finally figured out what that means, but I'm keeping quiet about it because I don't want to confuse you.

According to the experts Sam'l Johnson should be shipped back to the bush leagues forthwith. His letter was written on a sheet of lined greenish paper torn from a pad; he ignored such vital items as inside address and complimentary close. His spelling is atrocious, his punctuation nonexistent, and he wrote with a stubby pencil instead of an electric typewriter.

Yet, I'll bet you dollars to donuts Sam'l got *beter riting* by return mail. His letter lacked no important element; the $4 was enclosed, he stated what he wanted and gave instructions where to send the book. Everything else is a mere detail.

We aren't all Sam'l Johnsons, and we should attempt to follow a standard format when writing business letters. The point I am trying to make is that what is in the letter is the important factor. Letters should present a pleasing appearance to assure a favorable reception by the reader, but we are not going to spend our time or waste yours on a discussion of whether you should sign off with "Yours truly" or "Yours very truly" or whether you should or should not indent paragraphs. Let your secretary, who has attended an excellent business school, instruct you in these niceties.

What we will talk about briefly are a few of the principles governing the art of business letter writing.

Writing style

Why do executives write business letters? Let's consider that for a moment or two. We write because we have something to say: giving or asking for information or making a request for a decision or action. Buying, selling, complaining, or answering complaints—you name it, letters are written about it.

But why write a letter? Why not a phone call or a three martini lunch, provided a nondrinking junior is along to remember what was said or decided? Basically, it is a matter of logistics. You can lunch with only one group a day, and it becomes inconvenient if you are in Boston and your lunchmate is in San Diego. Then too, no one keeps minutes of a luncheon meeting, and six months later who remembers anything except that the Newcastle Potted Salmon hors d'oeuvre was overspiced with mace and cloves.

The telephone is a wonderful instrument, and dividends paid by Ma Bell have kept the wolf from the door of countless widows and orphans. But a phone call, like lunches, leaves no permanent record behind it.

Many business letters are written because writers need a record of the matters discussed in them. They should be written clearly so there will be no misunderstanding of the message. They should be concise and as short as possible.

Individuals who have no problem in talking over the phone or face to face with people often freeze when they write a letter. When that happens, the letter might begin like this: "In answer to your recent request I wish to advise that . . ." How do you prevent such a debacle? Simple. Imagine you are talking to the other person instead of writing to him. Tell him what you want to say in natural conversational English. Don't try to jazz up your writing so it becomes a formal, stilted treatise. To me, natural conversational English contains no coarseness, no jargon, and is grammatically and syntactically sound.

You would never think of opening a conversation with the sentence fragment quoted above. Read your letter aloud. How does it strike your ear? If you cringe when you hear what you have written, try it again.

Be natural, be clear, be concise.

Attitude

Be positive. Plunge in and tell it like it is. At the same time be polite, pleasant. Use active, not passive voice. (Twenty-two words that contain five suggestions. Succinct but not abrasive.)

Never be insensitive to the attitude and position of your reader. Try to see things from his point of view—answer his questions, show you have an understanding of his side of the matter. Don't stampede him.

Let us take a minute or two to think about the personality of words. When we talk face to face with someone, the words we use carry only a portion of the burden of communication. Facial expressions, gestures, inflections play an important role in transmitting our message. Remember Owen Wister's Virginian's warning, "When you say that, smile." We can see a smile, but we can't hear it over a telephone or detect it in a page of typescript. In writing, words carry the whole load. A friendly jibe in conversation may become an insult in writing as the reader cannot see the grin or catch the tone of voice that accompanied the crack.

So, be careful how you express yourself in writing. Read

the words you have written from the reader's point of view. Avoid sarcasm; don't be cute. Adopt a friendly yet dignified, courteous style.

Subject

It seems to me that it is only common sense to show the subject of a letter in the middle of the sheet directly above the *Dear Sir*. Underlining draws attention to it.

Subject: <u>Lease on Fifth Avenue Store</u>

Dear Sir:

The reader is prepared for what he will be reading, and perhaps the person who opens the mail might be motivated to attach the file to the letter before putting it on the boss's desk. Showing the subject is another way to make it easy for the reader and put him into a receptive frame of mind.

I have developed a great time saver in handling personal business correspondence. If I receive a request for information from my insurance broker, I type my reply in a blank area of his letter, make a copy at the office, paying my dime, of course, return the original to the broker and retain the copy for my file. Request and reply on the same piece of paper—unheard of. Businesses can't run that way, I suppose, but individuals can. On second thought, why shouldn't businesses handle at least part of their correspondence in such a manner? Unfortunately, I am unable to patent the process.

Believe it or not, but a few days ago I found myself in the middle of a sometimes acrimonious dispute whether *Subject* should appear above or below *Dear Sir*. The dispute was settled with a decision worthy of Solomon. If the writer preferred to list the subject above the salutation, he should do so, and should he wish to place it below, that was equally his perogative.

In other words, put the subject anywhere you please so long as you show it somewhere.

Dear Sir:, Dear Madam:, Gentlemen:, To Whom It May Concern:

Rule number one is: If you know the name of the person to whom you are writing, address him by name. Make your letter as personal as possible.

If you are writing to the unknown purchasing agent of a corporation, you should refer to him as *Dear Sir.* To call an individual *Gentlemen* would be inappropriate. Use *Gentlemen* when you are not directing your letter to any individual in an organization.

What do you do when a young friend who is job hunting asks you for a general recommendation? To start your letter *To Whom It May Concern* sounds awfully stilted. If you write *Dear Sir* and the personnel director happens to be a woman, your friend might not be treated with the warmth he deserves. Why not try *Dear Sir or Madam?*

At times the chairman of a corporation sends a letter to four hundred thousand stockholders and starts it *Dear Stockholders.* That sounds phony to me. I would much rather see the letter headed *To All Stockholders.*

Executives who are personal friends may use first names in correspondence provided the full name of the addressee appears in the address shown at the top of the letter and on the envelope. There is nothing wrong with starting a business letter *Dear George* and signing it with your given name. First names would not be used, however, if the letter involves legal matters or policy at a high level. In such cases a full signature is recommended.

Content

Why are you writing the letter? You should have a reason, and if you state it in the *Subject:* ... , your reader will at least know what you are writing about.

What points do you wish to make? They should be set forth in the first paragraph. Why beat around the bush? You are a busy man (we hope) and so is the person who will read your letter. Make your points clearly and tactfully, and if your letter calls for answers, be sure to state exactly what you want to know. Don't leave it to the addressee to figure out what information or decision you expect from him.

In taking such an approach a writer must be careful not to give an impression of Napoleonic arrogance. That is where tact comes in. It is possible to be direct without bulling about like an enraged African buffalo.

If you are a friend of the person to whom you are writing, don't start your letter with a reference to your Sunday golf game or Saturday's drunken brawl. Business letters should confine themselves to business matters. If you feel you should add a personal note, write it in your own hand at the bottom of the sheet.

Which brings up a different type of business letter. Let us say the bank you do business with sponsors an event on the PGA tour, and you were invited to play in the Pro-Am the day before the start of the tournament proper. To your delight you were paired with Hale Irwin, and you enjoyed the experience thoroughly. Your thank-you note to the bank officer responsible for your invitation is really a business communication, but it lists no subject, starts with *Dear Bill* and is written in an informal and personal vein. No strictly business matters should be tacked on to that letter.

Don't mix business and social matters. Keep them distinctly apart.

Sign your mail yourself

Not long ago a company in which I owned what I considered to be a substantial block of stock was purchased by a conglomerate at an exceptionally generous price. My profits were large, and with a feeling of sincere gratitude, I wrote the company president to compliment him on how well he had run the company and to thank him for his part in making my profits as large as they were. It was a damn good letter. Ten days later I received a reply, equally well written, friendly, appreciative, but beneath the signature, which was a model of penmanship with each letter clearly decipherable, appeared the initials S.P. The president had been too busy to sign his mail and had delegated that function to his secretary. Perhaps, even, she had composed the letter as well as signed it.

I am still grateful for the money the president made for me, but a stroke of his secretary's pen took all the pleasure out of the correspondence.

Situations may arise that prevent an executive from signing his mail. An unexpected trip, a sudden illness—these are legitimate excuses, but they can be handled without damage to the feelings of the recipient of the letter. The secretary types a note at the bottom of the page: "Mr. Blank, after dictating this letter, was unexpectedly called away but asked that I send it to you immediately." The initials L.S. appear under the boss's name and after the note.

When I receive the letter, I smile. Blank is a great guy—he's really concerned about me, and L.S., whoever she is, knows how to make a fellow feel good. The whole deal didn't take a minute, but what a difference it made.

So, sign your mail or explain why you don't. If you are too damn important to sign missives directed to such as I, malediction on you.

10

Business reports

A few million men and women write thousands of millions of words each year and brazenly call them business reports. If all the copies of these reports were stacked in a pile it would possibly girdle the globe twelve times at the equator or comfortably reach the moon. The paper staircase probably cost more to produce than the technology developed to put men on the moon if we include in expense not only writing time but also the reading time of the poor souls who must slog through the verbiage.

If a way could be found to cut reading volume by 25 percent, industry would save tens of millions of dollars a year. The solution is to teach people to write more clearly and concisely.

The remaining pages of the book will be devoted to this worthy cause and to expound a number of the basic rules of report writing.

Reports fit into one of two categories: action reports or expository reports.

The purpose of the action report is to inform, analyze, draw conclusions, and, most importantly, to recommend convincingly a specific course of action. On the other hand, an expository report merely sets forth the information and facts germane to an issue but makes no attempt to draw conclusions or propose action. By its nature an action report should be persuasive; an expository report should be coldly clinical with no attempt made to sway opinion.

The primary function of management is to make decisions and, based on them, to establish strategies designed to achieve chosen objectives. In our present society no executive of even a moderately large organization can be expected to know everything that is going on in his area of responsibility. Thus, he must rely to a considerable extent on reports submitted to him by his staff and his operating superintendents if his ultimate decisions are to be of the highest quality. Information given him as well as recommendations made to him must, therefore, be accurate, comprehensive; conclusions must be sound, realistic, and convincingly presented. Above all, recommendations should develop logically from the evidence on which they are based and be consistent with the situation as it exists rather than relate to the situation as it ought to be. In short, recommendations must be practical.

Steps in developing a report

No single established format has been agreed on for business reports. Every executive and organization sets ground rules covering the form a report should follow. Juniors must learn to adapt themselves to the idiosyncrasies and prejudices of bosses. If form is a constant variable, development of content is not.

The vast majority of action reports involves the following elements:

1. Collection and organization of material.
2. Analysis of the material.
3. Conclusions and recommendations based on the analysis.
4. Development of a specific course of action.

Each of these segments is important enough to deserve a paragraph or two.

Collection of material

When the big boss calls Charley to his office Monday morning and bellows, "Charley, what the hell's the matter with profits in the Three I territory last month?" the first thing Charley doesn't do is retort, "How the hell do I know." One does not address Pevley Clip, president and chief executive officer of Pin-Up Corporation, in such a manner if one enjoys his job and has aspirations to hold it a while longer.

Charley, with a sure instinct for self-preservation, tugs at his forelock and answers, "I'll find out and let you know."

"Do that," growls Clip, "and don't forget your recommendations. A week from today will be fine." A peremptory gesture dismisses Charley, and Clip returns to his study of the report that is engaging his attention at the moment.

Charley returns to his office and begins to think. His first job will be to secure a copy of the report that disclosed the dismal showing of the Iowa, Illinois, and Indiana division. He'll get that from Baynes Scattergood, general sales manager, who won't have any answers but will be smart enough to know he can't stonewall Clip's number one assistant. The next stop will be the Treasury Department. The Three I territory is a profit center, and a study of financial records will give Charley a clue as to how bad the situation really is. Eishade Waterhouse, the comptroller, will do all he can to satisfy Charley. He suffers from an inferiority complex, is mortally afraid of Clip, and will welcome an opportunity to do a favor for the agent of the old man.

Charley's mind is now hitting on all four. He'll call the division manager in Terre Haute, pick his brains, and secure permission from him to visit managers of the three or four hardest hit branches. Charley counts on his fingers, a habit he has never been able to break: Monday and Tuesday at the home office here in Shelbyville, three days in the field, the weekend at home organizing and writing the report—that gives him Monday morning for typing, editing, and putting the report in final shape. "Hell," he says to himself. "It's a cinch."

Charley may be young; self-confidence is his forte, and modesty is a characteristic foreign to his nature, but he is smart enough to know that only a fool tries to do anything strictly on his own. When he needs information, Charley pumps dry every source open to him, turns over all the rocks he can find, and ferrets around until he knows everything that is to be known on a subject.

Analysis of material

Back in Shelbyville, Charley starts to work on his analysis Saturday morning. All the information he has collected has been assembled under various headings. Among them are: manufacturing costs, marketing expense, unit sales, gross volume, competition, and general economic conditions. The answer, he is sure, will be found in one or more of these areas.

Manufacturing costs are well within budget—no problem there. Also, he notes no perceptible change in the economic environment; so those two elements can be, to a large extent, disregarded. Both will be dismissed in a sentence or two in his report. Why waste time flogging a dead horse?

Unit sales are spotty. They are down substantially in Iowa, up slightly in Illinois, and much higher in Indiana. Illinois shows a mixed pattern. The western part of the state had a serious drop, but sales around Chicago and the eastern part of the state were up. Charley gets a map of the Three I territory and color codes the performance of all the branches in the three states. The map will be an exhibit attached to his report. The sales pattern looks fishy.

Gross volume supplies a further clue. Revenues are way down in Iowa, weak in Illinois, and barely steady in Indiana despite the increase in unit sales.

Marketing expenses, higher across the board, supply another clue. Advertising has jumped dramatically in the whole territory, so have discounts given to distributors. The departure from normal in this account aroused Charley's suspicions as soon as he spotted it. Why such an increase?

Competition supplied the answer. On the first of the previous month, a mammoth mail-order house had cut the price on its competing clothespin, but, Charley had discovered, the reduction was limited to Iowa and a few contiguous counties in western Illinois. Other manufacturers, Pin-Up included, had met the price cut, and Pin-Up had also increased advertising allocations considerably in an attempt to maintain market share.

All right, but why increase advertising and cut prices in Illinois and Indiana where Pin-Up was encountering no unusual competitive pressure? Lash Monger, Three I division manager, had blown it. Meeting price competition in Iowa and a few counties in Illinois could possibly be defended, perhaps even increasing advertising, but what was the sense of extending the changes to the rest of the territory?

Charley worked on his analysis until he was confident he had covered every relevant issue. He then turned his attention to organizing the conclusions he had developed from his analysis.

Conclusions and recommendations

What alternative courses of action were available to Pin-Up? What other problems might ensue if the various strategies were adopted?

For instance, if special discounts to distributors in Indiana were discontinued at once, what would be the effect on sales for the next month or two? Charley had been around long enough to know that every action is accompanied by an equal and opposite reaction, and measurement of possible reaction was a must before any change in operation was made. He thought through the advantages and disadvantages of each of the strategies he had outlined and finally settled on the one that in his judgment had the best chance of extricating the division from the position it was in.

Course of action

Sunday morning Charley wrestled with remedial action and in the afternoon made his decision and wrote out the course of action he would recommend to Pevley Clip. The plan was set forth in detail. Who should do what was stated, when he should do it, and why it should be done was laid out in one, two, three, order so there could be no uncertainty on the part of anyone.

The evening was devoted to writing, editing, and rewriting the report. It would run to three typed pages plus two exhibits, and the draft would be ready for him before ten o'clock Monday, allowing time for last minute improvements before the finished report would be typed, checked for typographical errors, and submitted to the boss by noon.

Writing the report

Let us take a closer look at the steps Charley took as he prepared to write his report and how he handled the actual writing.

First, precisely what was his assignment? He wrote down Clip's exact words. "What the hell's the matter with profits in the Three I territory last month?" The scrap of paper was never out of sight or mind while Charley worked on the project. He knew from bitter experience that nothing must divert him from his primary objective—fulfilling his instructions. During his investigations he might discover that the manager of the Des Moines office had embezzled $80,000 of the company funds and the warehouse in Des Plaines contained, in addition to a few million clothespins, a cache of nine tons of marijuana. Both of these bits of information were important enough to be reported to the boss but were subjects not to be included in his present assignment unless they were factors in the profit decline in the Three.I territory.

Charley also kept the lowering visage of Pevley Clip constantly in his mind. He knew his boss's likes and dislikes as well as he knew those of his own wife. Clip couldn't abide rash assumptions—everything reported to him must be supported by evidence or reasoned conclusions. No one could con Pevley, and those who tried did so at the risk of instant dismissal. In addition, like others with Napoleonic complexes, Clip tolerated no familiarity from his underlings. Elephantine humor was his perogative alone; he freely ignored the rules of syntax and grammar in his speech but tolerated no slips by members of his staff. Profanity and slang in the mouths of others was an anathema to him, but his own speech was liberally dotted with "damns" and "hells." Clip was living proof of the validity of the theory of atavism; he was a spiritual and perhaps a lineal descendant of Genghis Khan, Attila the Hun, and Billy the Kid. Why did Charley work for him? For that matter why did anyone work for him? Charley had the answer. Clip was intensely loyal to those who played the game by his rules and predictable standards, and he rewarded them handsomely. He was a man from whom you could learn. Then, too, he was capable of unexpected acts of generosity. The previous winter Charley's wife had suffered a serious illness, and one morning shortly after her discharge from the hospital, Charley received a note from Clip ordering him to take her on a Caribbean cruise and enclosing a personal check that would more than cover all expenses.

Life around Pevley Clip wasn't a bed of roses, but it had its compensations. It is understandable why Charley was never unmindful of the personality of the man he was writing to.

Outline

Charley did not feel that making an outline of what his report would cover was beneath his dignity, and he went about its preparation exactly as he had been taught to do in sixth grade. He had learned that a detailed outline performed several important functions that aided him when he wrote a report.

When properly prepared, an outline assured a logical progression to the report. Points would follow in orderly sequence, and there would be no jumping about when he started to write. If the outline was followed rigidly—an essential requirement—it would eliminate the possibility of allowing himself to be trapped into irrelevant digressions. The outline would make it impossible to forget or ignore important issues once writing was underway. Finally, and by no means least importantly, the outline would supply the headings for each section of the report.

Knowing all this, Charley worked on his outline until he was satisfied it met his standards.

First draft

The next step was to flesh out the outline. The writing came surprisingly easy since he already had a framework for what he wanted to say. Charley was a fast writer and a wordy one, but this weakness did not worry him as he never considered the first draft to be even close to the finished product.

Editing

Charley did his writing on lined yellow sheets of paper he kept in a three-ring binder. He wrote only on the right-hand page, making minor corrections on the text itself, and using the left-hand page for major revisions. When the first draft had been carefully edited, a second draft was written, embodying all the changes made. Editing and rewriting continued until Charley was satisfied with the result.

Final draft

When the report was typed, Charley went over it still again as he had learned that weaknesses had a habit of showing up more clearly in type than in his crabbed handwriting. Once final corrections were made, the report received its final typing, and Charley checked it carefully once more to catch typographical errors and to make sure his figures were correctly copied.

At long last the report was ready for the eagle eyes of Pevley Clip.

General suggestions on report writing

The quality of recommendations made is of paramount importance and so is the specificity with which a course of action is set forth. Clear thinking is essential in writing a convincing report, and nothing can take the place of being right. Yet, many otherwise excellent reports are inferior to what they ought to be because the writer goes astray in one or more areas.

The start

Reports should begin this way:

Date:

To:
From:
Subject:

(Note: *To* always comes before *From*.)

Starting in this fashion is neither difficult nor intellectually demanding, but it is important. Problems start to pile up when the writer begins his first sentence. He will do well if he emulates Caesar who, as I recall from my brief study of him, was in the habit of plunging *in medias res.* His example is an excellent one. Don't start by describing the creation of the earth and continue to the present, eon by eon. Don't spend a page or two warming up the motor. As the tennis players and golfers do, a writer should ready himself before the match begins, and when the bell rings, he should be off and running. (An excellent example of mixed metaphors.)

Should Charley be asked to develop a price for a new product, an excellent beginning for his report would be: "I recommend a price of $12.85 each for silver-plated clothespins." Pevley Clip would respond favorably to such a beginning. He is given the recommendation immediately, and as he reads the report, he can test the analysis against the recommended price to see whether the argument is always consistent. On the other hand, if the price is withheld until the final paragraph, it is much more difficult for the reader to follow the trend of the analysis.

A report is not like a detective story in which the perpetrator of the dastardly deed is not unveiled until the final chapter when each of the clues is tied into the denouement by the brilliant deductions of the sleuth. Neither is it a cliffhanger in which the intrepid heroine plummets from crisis to crisis with monumental aplomb and an immaculate coiffure. There should be no dramatics in a report, no sudden revelations, no surprises.

Many executives, especially if a report is a long one, require that a half-page synopsis of the conclusions and recommendations be attached to the front of the report. This practice is particularly helpful when the problem is a complex one and the answer is not as simple as setting a price on a silver-plated clothespin.

Putting the recommendations up front is a good way for a writer to make it easy for his reader to follow and understand his argument.

Use of information

Across the nation rolls the report writer's plaintive wail, "I can't get enough information." At times this concern is real, and we'll get to it later, but far more problems are caused by a plethora of information than by a dearth of that commodity. Writers of reports at times feel an unquenchable urge to tell everything they know when they grip a no. 2 pencil and start writing. This tendency is aggravated if the boss is one of those benign souls who does not believe in stifling the creative and imaginative impulses of his assistant and neglects to impose a strict length limit on the report he has commissioned. It should be a matter of great interest to a reader to know that Sebastião José de Carvalho e melo, Marques do Pombal, 1699-1782, Portuguese statesman, expelled the Jesuits, curbed the Inquisition, reformed the schools, built up Brazil, and reconstructed Lisbon after the 1755 earthquake. Yet, what have these gems of information got to do with a marketing plan for Pin-Up's introduction of a new four-and-one-half-inch clothespin?

Researching a report unearths much more information

than a concise, well-written report can use. The writer's problem is what material to use and what to discard. Generally speaking, information germane to the issues being analyzed should be mentioned in a report. Data should be used to make sure a reader will have a sufficient background to understand a situation. It is also employed to support analysis and conclusions. All other information is redundant.

Assumptions

There is a vast distinction between a fact and an unsupported assumption, and a writer, if he is to earn the credibility of his reader, must clearly label his assumptions as assumptions and not try to pass them off as facts. It is essential to establish the validity and reasonableness of assumptions as fully as possible. Vehemence of language cannot overcome shallowness of argument. When a writer starts a sentence, "I am absolutely convinced that..." the reader usually suspects he is being conned. On the other hand if a writer makes an assumption and supports it with factual evidence and if the assumption then appears realistic, the reader can accept it not as a fact but as a reasonable probability. Many reports are unacceptably weak because of faulty and invalid assumptions.

Fiction writing

We are told that necessity is the mother of invention, and a review of the history of industrial production tends to support this adage. Invention, however, is not in the purview of the report writer. If a piece of evidence is missing, he cannot manufacture it. He cannot embroider on the truth. Imaginative approaches are to be applauded, but imagination and fabrication are not interchangeable qualities. Stay with the information you have or can secure, but don't substitute fiction for fact.

Not enough information

No one has ever had all the information he thinks he needs, and if the past is a valid indicator of the future, no one ever will. When the writer is confronted with a blank spot during research of an issue, he should ask himself why the missing information is necessary. Not infrequently, further study will result in the discovery that the information isn't as indispensable as it first appeared to be, but if it still seems required, he should ask himself how it could be obtained. What would be the cost in time and money to secure it? If the information were obtained, what could it show and what would be done dependent on what the information disclosed? It would then be necessary to make a decision whether or not to expend the time and money to locate the missing link. It is not adequate to take the attitude that since the information is not available, a writer may ignore what might be an important area.

Exhibits

The purpose of exhibits is to explain, clarify, support, and supplement the text of a report. Important facts disclosed by an exhibit should be stated in the text, which must stand independent of exhibits, so that it is not necessary to check exhibits for information developed in them but left hidden there and not mentioned in the text.

Exhibits, too, must be able to stand on their own and not require explanation in the text for full understanding. They should have proper headings, be complete, clear, and easily understandable should a reader study them before he reads the text of a report. Appending explanatory notes to exhibits so a reader can follow the methodology of their development is not only proper but desirable. To explain in the text how an exhibit is constructed is improper. Exhibits present facts and figures but no conclusions. These are reported only in the text.

Exhibits must provide the source of figures used in the report itself. Thus, if the text states, "Exhibit IV shows that fixed costs are $185,347," the exhibit should contain an itemized list of costs totaling that amount. The reader should not be forced to pick from the maze of figures in Exhibit IV a combination that reaches the desired total.

Executives are usually familiar with a number of different kinds of exhibits, and the skilled writer may use a variety of them in his reports. He will be expected to employ some or all of these types of exhibits.

1. *Figures.* Balance sheets, profit and loss statements, and so on. Many more figures can be shown on a report exhibit than should be included on a visual aid used in a presentation. It is not unusual to see five- or ten-year comparative financial statements on a single sheet. The only restriction on the amount of numbers is that they should not be too small for the eyes of myopic elderly directors. (See Exhibit I.)
2. *Line graphs.* Exhibit II is an illustration of this type of graph, which is an excellent means of showing progression of performance from period to period in a few selected accounts. Note that each line is clearly identified and the lines themselves are differentiated so that, should they happen to cross, there will be no confusion as to which is which. Line differentiation is superior to color coding if it is necessary to make several copies of the

exhibit and the copy equipment does not reproduce in color.

Line graphs are not as precise as columns of figures. A study of Exhibit II reveals that profits in 1977 were slightly over $7 million and dividends were approximately $4.2 million. To enter the precise amounts for each year on the graph would congest it to such an extent its value would be lost. The same would be true if retained earnings, income taxes paid, and research and development costs were charted on the same graph.

3. *Bar graphs.* Exhibit III is a simple example of a bar graph. It shows only gross sales, is uncluttered and easy to understand. In this instance vertical bars are used. They can also be drawn horizontally. A report might refer to this graph thusly: "Exhibit III shows that sales have increased sevenfold between 1972 and 1979." You will note that the vertical axis (dollar volume) starts at zero and that the bars are of equal width.

Exhibit IV is totally unacceptable as it contains two serious and deceptive flaws. The information it conveys should be identical with that contained in the last half of Exhibit III, but the impression on the viewer is entirely different. Part of this deception is caused by the vertical axis (dollar volume) starting at $50 million instead of zero. The increase from about $56 million sales in 1976 to $80 million in 1979 is 43 percent, a handsome rise to be sure, but it appears to be a great deal more than that on the graph. Also, the 1979 bar is four times as wide as the 1976 bar. If my mathematics is (are?) correct, the area of the 1979 bar is 23 times the area of the 1976 bar; yet the sales represented by the 1979 bar are less than twice the 1976 sales. Dirty pool. Pevley Clip would fire you forthwith and good riddance.

Bars should be of the same width, scales should start at zero, and don't you dare to forget it!

4. *Pie charts.* See Exhibit V. These are effective when showing percentages that should add up to 100. Government and corporate reports are full of them. They tell us how every dollar received is spent, what portion of our food bill goes for groceries, meat, dairy products, beer and hard liquor. Two problems arise when pie charts are constructed. If several segments are small, how do you label them? Writing sideways on the chart is hard to read, and a number of arrows pointing to mother-in-law slivers isn't good either. The other problem is mechanical. Twelve percent of a circle is 43.2 degrees. If you can mark off 43.2 degrees of arc, more power to you. If you can't, get someone who can or use a different kind of chart.

5. *Map graphs.* Refer to Exhibit I in Chapter 3, "Presentations," for an example of this type of exhibit. Maps are a great help when readers are asked to visualize a geographic area. They must, however, be well drawn and accurate. Don't clutter the map with too much writing. Use shading, numbers, and letters with the keys printed below the map.

6. *Organization charts.* Instead of spending a page describing who reports to whom or where the director of stockholder relations fits into the corporate hierarchy, why not draw an organization chart and call it Exhibit VI. Many times it helps to show the names of the individuals who occupy the boxes.

7. *Floor plans—Flowcharts.* A well-drawn floor plan of a proposed factory will impress the board more than a thousand descriptive words. Often the flow of material through a shop can be dramatically presented by showing the path it takes from department to department as it is being converted from raw material to finished product.

(I must apologize. I had intended to use as an exhibit a plan of Pin-Up's new Shelbyville plant which shows how fourteen-inch logs are fabricated into clothespins in a continuous operation lasting only fifty-seven minutes; however, Pevley Clip confiscated the exhibit on the grounds it might divulge to the competition the secret methods of manufacturing that had made Pin-Up the leader in the clothespin industry.)

8. *Glyphs.* I'll bet you never heard of them. I hadn't until I read about the little things in a book. A glyph is a symbolic figure or character, a scratching. Thus, when I ask if you know what a glyph is, I should scribble a doodle after the question, ⟨??⟩ , and I have made a glyph.

"Profits were down last year. ☹ They will be up this year." ☺ The author of the book exhorted his readers to use glyphs in visual aids prepared for speeches, to include them in exhibits and even to scatter them through the text of a report to lighten the atmosphere with a bit of humor. In my judgment he is a glyphomaniac, and though I am indebted to him for teaching me a new word, the three glyphs I have drawn will be my total production lifetimewise.

It is undesirable to have to turn a page sideways to read an exhibit, but sometimes this is unavoidable, as in Exhibits I and VI. Long sheets of paper are a pain in the neck for a reader to handle and so are exhibits that unfold to a width of a couple of feet and, like roadmaps, are impossible to refold in original creases. Both exhibits and reports should be written on the same size paper.

Properly used, exhibits can be substantial word savers,

EXHIBIT I
PIN-UP CORP.
Balance Sheets
($000)

Assets	12/31/75	12/31/76	12/31/77	12/31/78	12/31/79
Cash	$ 73	$ 71	$ 346	$ 140	$ 94
Accounts receivable	246	336	221	217	282
Inventories and prepaid expenses	1,104	675	558	652	816
Total Current Assets	$1,423	$1,082	$1,125	$1,009	$1,192
Fixed assets less depreciation	217	223	220	221	214
	$1,640	$1,305	$1,345	$1,230	$1,406

Liabilities and Owners' Equity	12/31/75	12/31/76	12/31/77	12/31/78	12/31/79
Payables and accruals	$ 562	$ 280	$ 249	$ 169	$ 199
Refunds due customers	63	63	63	63	67
Accrued income taxes	24	38	40	40	40
Notes payable to banks and others	344	251	68	31	181
Total Current Liabilities	$ 993	$ 632	$ 420	$ 303	$ 487
Long-term notes payable	18	27	271	265	252
Total Liabilities	$1,011	$ 659	$ 691	$ 568	$ 739
Owners' equity	629	646	654	662	667
	$1,640	$1,305	$1,345	$1,230	$1,406

which may be important when there is a rigid limit to the
length of a report.

Exhibits should be numbered in the order they are mentioned in the text. Reference to them may be made in two
ways: "Exhibit I shows an estimated ..." or "Profits of
$100,000 are projected (Exhibit II)." Use Roman numerals
when identifying exhibits. Exhibits should not be scattered
through the text but should be grouped together at the end
of the report.

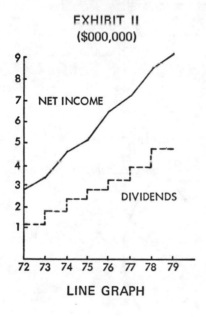

EXHIBIT II
($000,000)

NET INCOME

DIVIDENDS

LINE GRAPH

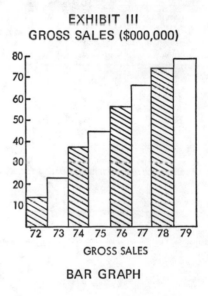

EXHIBIT III
GROSS SALES ($000,000)

GROSS SALES

BAR GRAPH

EXHIBIT IV
GROSS SALES ($000,000)

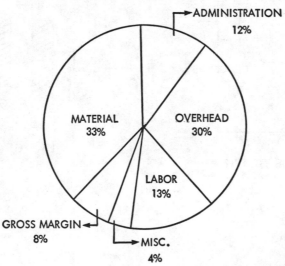

BAR GRAPH

EXHIBIT V
FACTORY COSTS, 1979

PIE CHART

EXHIBIT VI
Stewart Hardware Company, Inc., Organization chart

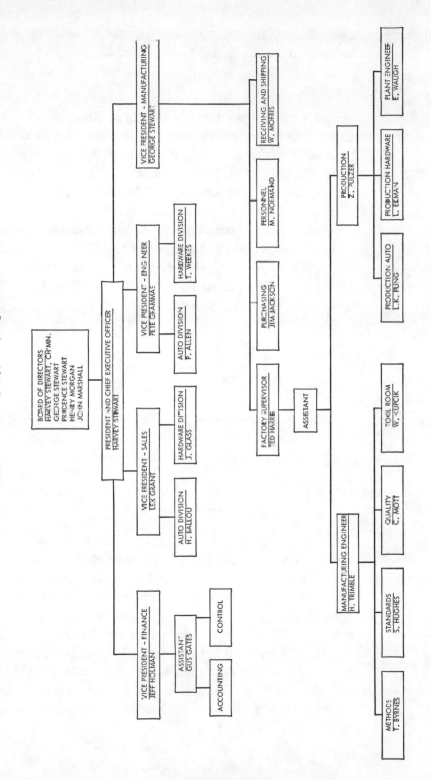

BOARD OF DIRECTORS
HARVEY STEWART, CH'MN.
GEORGE STEWART
PRUDENCE STEWART
HENRY MORGAN
JOHN MARSHALL

PRESIDENT AND CHIEF EXECUTIVE OFFICER
HARVEY STEWART

VICE PRESIDENT - FINANCE
JEFF HOLMAN

ASSISTANT
GUS GATES

ACCOUNTING

CONTROL

VICE PRESIDENT - SALES
LEX GRANT

AUTO DIVISION
H. BALLOU

HARDWARE DIVISION
J. GLASS

VICE PRESIDENT - ENGINEER
PETE CHAMMAS

AUTO DIVISION
P. ALLEN

HARDWARE DIVISION
T. WEEKES

VICE PRESIDENT - MANUFACTURING
GEORGE STEWART

FACTORY SUPERVISOR
TED HARRE

PURCHASING
JIM JACKSON

PERSONNEL
M. NOFMAND

RECEIVING AND SHIPPING
W. MORRIS

ASSISTANT

MANUFACTURING ENGINEER
H. TRIMBLE

PRODUCTION
Z. PULZER

METHODS
T. BYRNES

STANDARDS
S. HUGHES

QUALITY
C. MOTT

TOOL ROOM
W. KUPCIK

PRODUCTION-AUTO
L.K. FUNG

PRODUCTION HARDWARE
L. EEMAN

PLANT ENGINEER
E. WAUGH

First things first

Don't get bogged down in details and nonessentials at the expense of ignoring major areas. A judicious use of an outline will aid a writer in avoiding this trap. Pin-Up's market has been seriously eroded by the increasing popularity of home dryers, and the company is considering the introduction of a silver-plated metallic pin in an attempt to dominate the top segment of the market. Pevley Clip instructs one of his assistants to write a report on the feasibility of the project. Amos Singlefoot shuns the assistance of an outline in organizing his report and assigns weights and values to the issues involved in these proportions:

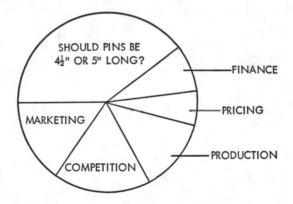

If we are charitable, we can say that Amos has sliced his pie all wrong. He has his priorities rear end up. The length of the pins is a detail, and it is debatable if Pin-Up will experience any substantial competition should it proceed with the project. On the other hand, it would appear that a market study of the proposal is essential. Will people buy silver-plated clothespins at the recommended price of $12.85 each? Indeed, is that the right price? How many does Pin-Up expect to sell? Can that number be turned out without upsetting production schedules of standard items? Is the company able to finance the new line? What is a realistic projection of the results in the first year? These are some of the basic questions that must be answered before design, sales, and production argue about the critical half-inch of length.

Some major areas may be covered adequately in a few sentences while less important issues might require more explanation. Exhibits can be most helpful in cutting down demands for space in a report. Balance is the essential ingredient when a report is blocked out in the planning stage.

Consistency

Conclusions should flow from analysis, not move counter to it. A report should be internally consistent so that a statement made on page one is not reversed later on.

"Amos Singlefoot debauched my teen-aged sister, purloined the family silver from his widowed and destitute mother, and burned the county poorhouse causing the deaths of forty senile octogenarians."

Three pages later the following sentence appears: "Amos Singlefoot is a man of integrity, possesses a sterling character and is guided by the highest principles of ethical and moral conduct."

Note: The reason Amos is no longer a member of Pevley's personal staff or even an employee has nothing to do with certain irregularities of his character but because Clip held him responsible for the silver-plated pin debacle. Pevley's motto has always been "First things first."

Ignoring the negative

Accentuating the positive is an admirable characteristic of personal behavior, but it is not always the best policy in business circles. All too often a writer sweeps under the rug whatever unpleasant facts he happens upon if he finds they are not compatible with his neat and comfortable analysis and conclusions. He is prone to acknowledge only what supports his argument and ignore whatever does not. This tendency often results from arriving at a faulty conclusion.

In the best of all possible worlds a recommendation conceivably might fit all known facts and considerations. In our imperfect society, however, this will seldom occur, and trade-offs of various magnitude will be inevitable. For example, Pin-Up's decision to make silver-plated clothespins may be fully compatible with the company's capabilities with the exception that $800 will have to be expended to run new power lines to the plating tanks. This expense is acceptable when related to the expected profits of the project, but if it becomes evident that a new building must be constructed at a cost of $2 million to house the operation, that would put an entirely different complexion on the matter.

Even if the expenditure were determined to be economically sound, the question of the availability of the $2 million would have to be explored. Has Pin-Up the necessary cash or can it borrow it? If the money can be obtained, is this the best possible use for it? All these questions would have to be answered before the final decision is made.

It does not pay to see only what you want to see and to consider only what reinforces your argument. Should there be too many loose ends left dangling and a number of embarrassing unanswered questions that must be ignored, the alarm buzzer should sound, and the writer should reexamine the validity of his analysis and conclusions.

Another ploy often used to get around a sticky point goes like this: "Since I have no information on factory capacity, I will assume Pin-Up has the facilities necessary to silver-plate three thousand clothespins an hour." The sentence makes innocuous reading, but the writer who attempts to whisk it by the nose of Pevley might find himself in the plating tanks along with his clothespins.

Breadth of analysis

There is a law of nature to the effect that every action is accompanied by an equal and opposite reaction. Also, there is a saying, the details of which are unclear to me, concerning irresistible forces and immovable objects. All this leads to the fact that when something happens, something else has got to give. Thus, when a business decision is made, the course of action undertaken may have a substantial effect on seemingly nonrelated matters.

For example, Pin-Up's plating tanks will be filled to capacity for ninety days with the new plated pins, and it will be impossible to platinum plate the twelve dozen gross of kitchen matches ordered by the Emir of Qhat, who will use them as a bribe to lure a French chef from the employ of the Maharajah of Rawalpindi. Failure to fill the Emir's order in timely fashion will possibly cause his cousin, the Caliph of Quot, to break off negotiations on the purchase of solid gold walking sticks for the twenty-two fathers of his forty-six wives.

It is essential to appraise the effect any decision might have on other activities of a company. Whether or not Pin-Up should produce silver-plated pins is an issue that must be evaluated in relation to the whole situation of the company. Much more is involved than the pins themselves.

Avoid superficiality. Analyze in depth and deal in specifics. There may be a single major component in a problem, but it is most unlikely that only a single issue needs to be handled. Don't limit coverage too narrowly. Breadth and depth of analysis are essential. The writer should develop his perception so he can see the whole situation, not just one narrow segment. The one-shot approach is usually the wrong one.

No decision can be made in a vacuum. The solution of one problem often creates other problems that must also be solved. Leander Wigglesworth, foreman of the plating department, demands an air-conditioned office so he can escape the malodorous fumes emanating from one of his plating tanks. It is given to him, and the day he moves in, seventeen other foremen petition for equal treatment.

Decisions should take into consideration the implications inherent in the recommended action. A broad view is necessary, and qualities of sensitivity and perception must be developed in order to anticipate the new problems that will arise so that solutions to them will be found along with the solution to the original problem. No problem or issue is an island unto itself.

Proof by mathematics

Very often a writer, carried away by his rhetoric and lost in a maze of mathematical computations of his own creation, reaches conclusions that are totally unrealistic. The mathematics may be perfect, but they might project a result that is ridiculous. Such an unfortunate situation arises when assumptions and analytical processes are basically unsound. Always examine decisions in the cold, hard light of common sense.

Let us assume that Pin-Up intends to test-market its silver-plated clothespins in Tupelo, Mississippi, and the adjacent area, which would include the teeming metropolises of Shannon, Fulton, Okolona, and Pontotoc. Let us also suppose that the gross margin per silver-plated pin is 85 cents and the costs of the special introductory program including advertising, promotion, special sales efforts, and substantial discounts to retailers add up to $963,333. Mathematics tells us that Pin-Up must sell 1,133,333 silver-plated pins to break even. No one can dispute the accuracy of the computations, but mastery of the fundamentals of addition, subtraction, multiplication, and division cannot alter the fact that the 19,000 men, women, and children of Tupelo, plus about another 20,000 in the outer environs of the city would each have to purchase twenty-nine clothespins at $12.85 each for Pin-Up to meet its break-even point. It is highly probable that a number of children under the age of six, even if they had the necessary $372.65, would forego the purchase of silver-plated pins in favor of a Superman costume and two thousand dozen pieces of bubble gum.

Every conclusion should be tested against the hard facts of life. Any projections or course of action must be reasonable and realistic

Reasonable

What is reasonable? What is realistic? Is it a matter of personal intuitive judgment, a product of experience? "It is reasonable to expect a 5 percent increase in sales." "A cost increase of 4 percent is to be expected." "Historically, earnings have increased at 6 percent per annum, and it is reasonable to expect this trend to continue." All this is very persuasive. Who can argue about a modest 4 percent, 5 percent, or 6 percent? Any normal person would accept that on faith. Not so!

Remember this: nothing happens unless something is done to cause it to happen. Pin-Up's silver-plated clothespins won't sell themselves even at 25 cents each. Some action must take place before a single pin is sold. Nothing is reasonable or realistic by fiat. It must be demonstrated to be reasonable or realistic before we can accept the conclusion. Reasonableness must be determined by analysis, not mandate.

Decision making

There is no place in reports for vague generalizations. Statements should be definite, specific, and must be clearly and precisely presented. "In order to meet corporate goals, Pin-Up must develop a strong marketing program." Such a statement is valueless unless the writer lays out in detail his "strong" plan. Specificity is essential. Who is to do what, when will he do it, and exactly how will it be done? A writer must be convincing and willing to take full responsibility for his decision. Decision is the name of the game, and an unwillingness to commit oneself wholeheartedly to a course of action is tantamount to abdication of the responsibilities and privileges of management.

Some persons are constitutionally unable to reach a decision and then act on it. To them there are not two sides to every question, but perhaps a dozen, and there is so much to be said in support of each approach that it is impossible to choose one above all the others. Such persons will undoubtedly find more happiness and success in philosophic milieus than as sales executives for Pin-Up Corporation.

In business the best decision or course of action is not always determinable. No man can bat a thousand in any league. As a matter of fact, not since 1941 has a major leaguer batted .400, and even then Ted Williams made out three times for every two hits he made. The main thing is he got the bat off his shoulder and took his cuts when he faced a pitcher. If an executive cannot be expected always to make the best decision, at least he can be expected not to make the worst, and as his perception and experience broaden, the quality of his decisions should improve. Don't be afraid to put your neck on the line. That is what necks are for, and how else can you expect to sell silver-plated clothespins?

Don't be afraid to make a mistake. Mistakes are normal and expected events, even in Pin-Up and other superlatively run companies. Strive for a good batting average, and let the chips fall where they may; however, the successful executive is perceptive enough to see a mistake soon after it has been made, man enough to acknowledge it, and capable enough to correct it before it destroys his company and himself.

Making decisions in reports is difficult because the writer goes on record, and he is aware his mistakes will return to haunt him. Consequently, his analysis must be complete, sound, and in depth so that the odds of being right are as much in his favor as he can make them.

Being convincing and at the same time honest

A report must be forceful, persuasive, and conclusive. Your analysis and recommendations may be absolutely perfect, but if your readers are not convinced, your recommendations will probably be ignored. Thus, it is not only what you say that is important but also how you say it. Style, organization of material, clarity, succinctness of expression, word choice— all these elements are factors in establishing credibility. Beautiful expression, however, cannot compensate for shallowness of argument. For best results, a combination of good form and sound analysis is recommended.

Reports generally are persuasive. The writer analyzes a situation and decides on the course of action he considers to be the best solution to the problem. Believing in the validity of his solution, he does his utmost to convince his readers to do what he recommends. If he is to earn a reputation for credibility and reliability, he must be scrupulously honest in every word he writes. Total honesty is an absolute requisite.

We have talked about unsupported assumptions regarded as facts, ignoring facts that do not fit into a solution, reaching unrealistic conclusions, and several other elements that weaken reports. Actually, many of these have to do with the personal integrity of the writer. Even though he may not be aware he is being less than candid, the effect of his faulty analysis may convince his reader to do something that is not in his best interest.

A writer must never fail to be aware of his responsibility to be honest and straightforward.

Pragmatism

Pin-Up's pugnacious panjandrum, Pevley Clip, prides himself on his no-nonsense attitude. Excerpts from his recent speech to the McMinnville Lions Club were printed in the local *Clarion*. " 'Show me' is my slogan," Mr. Clip stated. "When someone tries to con me into something, I ask three questions: 'Says who? So what? Is that really so?' In my shop nobody, not nobody, pulls the wool over my eyes. I point the horny finger at them and they better have the right answers." The reporter added that as Mr. Clip roared these words, he extended his right arm stiffly and pointed his forefinger, curved like the cruelly hooked beak of a turkey bustard, at his cringing audience.

Adoption of Pevley's attitude, if not his manner, can prove rewarding to all managers. Report writers, especially if their boss is a man like Clip, will be wise to make sure every statement they make is accurate, fully substantiated, clear and realistic. At the same time their argument should be consistent and directed at the issues under discussion.

Risk

Decisions usually involve both rewards and risks. Swinging the bat is necessary if your desire is to hit a home run. At the same time, the batter cannot ignore the possibility he might strike out. Business executives are often extremely adept in evaluating the benefits that should accrue from a recommended course of action, but the most successful of them never ignores the risk side of the question. He asks and answers these questions: What could go wrong? What would be the cost if it did? How could the damage be controlled? What remedial action could be taken? Above all, he must have a realistic understanding of the probabilities of success or failure.

Amos Singlefoot might forecast $100,000 profit from silver-plated pins in the first year, but hard-nosed, pragmatic Pevley might decide there is only a 10 percent chance of this happening, whereas there is a 90 percent chance Pin-Up would lose up to $1 million on the project. The decision is reduced to an analysis of reward, exposure, probability. No report writer should fail to evaluate the risks involved when he recommends a course of action.

Last words in this chapter

At this time I have an almost irresistible urge to gather all the pearls of wisdom scattered so profusely through the preceding pages into a summary of startling clarity and brilliance. Remembering that reiteration is redundancy, I conquer the impulse and close with the last paragraph of the final report written to Clip by Amos Singlefoot. A small company was up for sale and Clip asked Amos for specific recommendations covering: Should Pin-Up make an offer to buy and, if so, how high should Pin-Up be prepared to go.

The following quotation is the conclusion of the report.

The important things to keep in mind when making your decision are: Clothes Horse is making a good profit and should continue to do so in the future: the price seems to be about right for the business: the dollar investment is well within your means, and there is every reason to believe that you can make a healthy return on this investment. This is as far as I can go, Mr. Clip: the rest is up to you.

When he finished reading, Pevley was so enraged he jotted down nine excerpts and noted his comments on each. He added a short note and sent the handwritten sheet and the report to Charley Lightfoot.

your decision — I asked for his decision

good profit — How big is good?

should continue — Perhaps it should. Will it?

Price seems to be about right — What price? Why does it seem right? What does about mean?

Well within your means — What are our means?

Every reason to believe — Not one reason not to believe?

Healthy return — What is healthy? $ + $ is what I want.

As far as I can go — He hasn't gone anywhere, yet.

Rest is up to you — Rest of it? He means all of it.

Immediate Action!

Charley—
Fire him. Pull whatever strings you have to but get him a top job with the competition. Having him working against us instead of for us guarantees a 10% increase in our share of market. Cliff

11

Producing a report

For quite a while we have been talking about report writing, and it's time for us to produce one. Unfortunately, Pevley Clip refuses to allow us to push our proboscis into Pin-Up's affairs, so we will devote our attention to an issue that Gold Nugget feels is essential to settle.

Patrick Callaghan, a young man with a dozen years experience in the mining industry, had recently joined Gold Nugget as director of development and planning. One morning Joe Marlow, vice-president of the ore processing plant, called Patrick to his office and gave him an assignment.

"We've got to do something about disposing of our acid sludge," he said. "We've been kicking the problem around for months, and I've just got a cost estimate on a construction program. Here's my file on the situation. Read it, talk to anyone you want, and give me a report within a week. Let me offer a word of advice. Keep it short and sweet. Use all the exhibits you feel are necessary, but hold the text to not more than 800 words. And," he added, "no pussyfooting. Tell me what we should do and why. Got that?"

"Yes, sir." Patrick picked up the file and returned to his office to study it.

As usual he didn't have all the information he needed. Some of it he picked up in the ensuing two days. Other bits and pieces were unobtainable, and in those areas he had to rely on his judgment and analytical skill. One fact he had already known: Gold Nugget would have no difficulty finding the cash needed for the construction program if it was decided the new plant should be built.

Inserted here is a digest of the information Callaghan collected.

Gold Nugget, Inc., was a large vertically integrated mining operation which owned a number of mines, a metallurgical processing plant, and had its own sales division. In the processing plant the rough ore shipped from the mines was cleaned, purified, mixed with alloys when necessary, and shaped into bars, ingots, sheets, and so on, for storage and ultimate sale. Many of the processes, especially those of cleaning and purifying, employed large quantities of acid and operated seven days a week, 365 days a year. Gold Nugget's present annual acid consumption was 12,000 short tons and was increasing 2 percent to 3 percent yearly.

The cleaning and purifying processes generated an acid sludge refuse which had up to now been dumped in various abandoned mines and rock quarries owned by the company. Because of limited capacity and increasing environmental restrictions, Gold Nugget was soon going to have to find some other way of disposing of its sludge.

There were two methods commonly employed throughout the industry to handle similar waste problems. One was to ship the sludge back to the acid manufacturer, who then reprocessed the sludge and reclaimed the acid for commercial use. This method would cost Gold Nugget the lost value of the reclaimed acid, freight charges, occasional tank cleaning charges, and demurrage charges if the acid plant could not immediately accept the shipment. The additional charges could run up to 25 percent of the average monthly bill for freight alone. It was expected that the regular freight charges would average about $1,000 a month. This method had the advantage, however, that it involved no change in the present plant, and once out the door, the sludge was a problem for someone else.

The second method was to build a reconversion plant for the

sludge. Land adjacent to Gold Nugget's processing plant was already owned, and the technology had been perfected over the years. The cost of a plant with a capacity of 100 tons of sludge per day (the most economic unit) and a life of 20 years was projected to be approximately $1 million plus an additional capital expenditure of $250,000 for internal changes in the processing plant in order to adapt it to the new waste handling system. Cost of operation would vary with capacity utilization, and some retraining of personnel would be necessary.

Percent utilization	Cost per ton of sludge processed
25%	$28
50	24
75	20
100	16

These costs included all factory charges except depreciation and the renovation expense of the processing plant. The new plant would render 50 percent of the sludge into reusable acid which would represent 75 percent of the original acid used in the process. Thus, the company would be dependent on outside supplies for only 25 percent of its acid requirements, which, given the current inflationary price structure, was considered to be a definite advantage of this system. Another advantage was the deacidified sludge was easily disposed of as ecologically safe landfill at no further cost to the company.

Average price of acid—Delivered at plant

1970	$33.60
1971	34.25
1972	35.00
1973	36.00
1974	37.50
1975	40.50

1976	....	44.00
1977	....	48.50
1978	....	53.50
1979	....	58.50

As he studied his notes, Patrick was somewhat apprehensive about his position. He wanted to make a good showing on the assignment, but to do so he would have to put his neck squarely on the chopping block when he made his recommendations. Even though he was new with the company, he was director of planning and development, and it was his responsibility both to plan and direct. So be it. He'd give the job his best shot and take his chances on being right.

Once he had mastered all the available information, Patrick prepared an outline for his report. Following a long-established habit, he started with a statement of the assignment so it would never be far from his eyes.

After several revisions the outline looked like this:

GOLD NUGGET

Assignment: <u>Recommend course of action for sludge disposal. 800 words.</u>

OUTLINE

I. External influences on Gold Nugget
  A. Inflation
    1. Acid price
    2. Building costs
  B. Economic and environmental considerations
    1. Gov't regs. getting tougher
    2. Little likelihood of relief

II. Alternatives
   A. Do nothing
      1. No good. Must get answer to disposal problem.
   B. Return sludge to manufacturer
      1. Develop costs
      2. Does relieve G. N. of responsibility for sludge
      3. What if:
         a. Mfg. refuses delivery
         b. Strike at Mfg. or on R.R.
         c. Acid prices rise at faster rate than projected
      4. Backward step toward goal of self-sufficiency
   C. Build reconversion plant
      1. Develop costs
      2. Possible difficulties in construction or operation
      3. Compatibility with implicit co. objectives
   D. Cost analysis
      1. Alternative B v. C
   E. General considerations
      1. Availability of needed funds
      2. Is this an economic use of funds
      3. What if co. is forced to build plant later
      4. Are projected acid cost increases accurate
III. Decision
   A. Build plant immediately

Patrick's next step was to write the first draft of his report. He knew Marlow was fully aware of the general situation, and it would be a mistake to rehash all the material on the issue. Besides, he had only 800 words at his disposal. Facts would be used only to support his analysis and conclusions. Mathematical computations would be contained in exhibits, and conclusions drawn from them would appear in the text of the report.

Callaghan's fourth and final draft read like this:

January 15, 1980

To: Executive Committee
From: Patrick Callaghan
Subject: Disposition of Acid Sludge Refuse

I recommend Gold Nugget construct a sludge reconversion plant immediately at a total cost of $1,250,000.

Inflation

The price of acid has risen from $33.60 a ton in 1970 to $58.50 in 1979. In the last two years cost has increased $5 a year. If this trend continues, the price will approximate $78.50 by 1983. (See Exhibit I.)

Building costs are rising also. Plant construction plus alterations required will total $1,250,000 if work is started now. Delay will result in substantial cost increases.

Predicting the actual rate of inflation over the next five years is impossible, but costs are not expected to drop or even level off in the present economic environment.

Ecological and environmental considerations

Regulatory authorities have been stiffening requirements. Despite pressures resulting from the energy shortage, unfavorable publicity arising from indiscriminate dumping of wastes in the past makes it unlikely restrictions will be relaxed.

Alternatives open to Gold Nugget

A. Do nothing. This is not a realistic solution since a new way must be found to dispose of sludge in a manner compatible with stiffer regulations. It would not be wise for us to attempt to force relaxation of requirements by legal action. Even if successful, unfavorable publicity would harm the company image.

B. Return sludge to manufacturer. This alternative has the advantage of relieving Gold Nugget of responsibility after the sludge is shipped out. However, we would suffer if the manufacturer refused delivery or if a strike on the manufacturer or the railroad prevented shipments to or from our plant.

In addition, having no capacity for self-sufficiency, we would be completely at the mercy of the manufacturer that would be our only source of acid.

Exhibit II projects costs for this alternative for the years 1980 through 1983. It indicates costs will increase from about $800,000 in 1980 to more than $1 million in 1983. If acid prices rise more than the projected $5 a year, total costs will reach an even higher figure.

C. Build a conversion plant. Exhibit III shows projected costs for operating the plant to be $880,000 in 1981, $910,000 in 1982, and $940,000 in 1983. It is anticipated the plant would not be in operation until 1981.

Under this alternative Gold Nugget would be in a vulnerable position if the plant should break down or if unusual or unexpected costs or delays affect the new plant. However, since the technology of the reconversion process has been proven and since we have had extensive experience in ore processing, there is little reason for anticipating abnormal difficulties getting the plant started. We could purchase larger amounts of acid if a prolonged breakdown occurred in the reconversion process.

We are a large vertically integrated company, and construction of the plant is compatible with an implicit corporate objective of self-sufficiency.

Analysis

Exhibit IV is based on Exhibits II and III and projects costs of both alternatives through 1986. Granted the projected increase in acid price, relative profitability of the conversion plant will increase at a rapid pace since only 25 percent of acid needs would have to be purchased. This is primarily because cost of reclaimed acid, about $48 a ton in 1981 (see Exhibit V) compares with projected $68.50 cost of purchased acid. As price of purchased acid increases, the cost differential will widen still further.

Of course, should acid price drop below $48, the company would be worse off. Yet, probability of a substantial price drop is much less than the probability of continued price increases.

General considerations

The $1,250,000 needed for construction and alteration can be taken either from cash on hand or borrowed. Exhibit VI compares operations under the two alternatives. With cost of capital charged at 12 percent, the exhibit indicates the conversion plant will show an advantage of only $175,000 in its first three years of operation. Based on this alone it would not be wise to build the plant, but the savings of $570,000 projected for the next three years alters the picture.

Building the plant will answer the sludge disposal problem as residue from the reconversion process can be used as ecologically safe fill.

Every year of delay will see an increase in acid price and construction costs. We may also anticipate no easing of ecological regulations. The major uncertainty concerns the extent of acid price rise. To assume a substantial steady rise is to take a calculated risk, yet I feel that it is more probable that prices will continue to rise than that they will fall. Even should there be no financial advantage in building the plant, I would still recommend its construction as it will relieve our present total dependence on outside sources for supplies of vital importance to us.

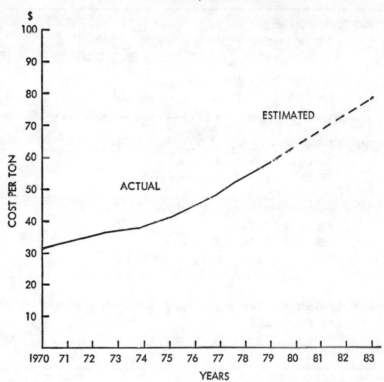

EXHIBIT I
Acid cost per ton

EXHIBIT II
Dollar costs if sludge is returned to manufacturer

1980	Freight cost per month	$1,000		
	Additional costs	250		
		$1,250	$	15,000 P/A
	Acid cost $63.50 (Ex. I)			
	Tons 12,300 (2½% increase)			781,050
	Total		$	796,050
1981	Freight plus 2½%			15,375
	Acid cost $68.50 (Ex. I)			
	Tons 12,607 (2½% increase)			863,579
	Total		$	878,954
1982	Freight plus 2½%			15,760
	Acid costs $73.50 (Ex. I)			
	Tons 12,922 (2½% increase)			949,767
	Total		$	965,527
1983	Freight plus 2½%			16,155
	Acid cost $78.50 (Ex. I)			
	Tons 13,245 (2½% increase)			1,039,732
	Total			$1,055,887

Assumptions:
Acid cost will continue to increase at rate of $5 per year.
Consumption will increase at rate of 2½ percent per year.

EXHIBIT III
Projected dollar costs if plant is built and in operation in 1981

Plant construction	$1,000,000
Alterations	250,000
	$1,250,000
Depreciation—20 years	$ 62,500 P/A
Cost of money at 12%	$ 150,000 P/A

Year	Item	Cost	
1981	Depreciation	$ 62,500	
	Cost of money	150,000	
	Acid needs one fourth of 12,607 tons,		
	3,152 tons at $68.50	215,912	
	Sludge conversion:		
	12,607 × 1.5 = 18,910 × $23.85*	451,003	
	Total		$879,415
1982	Depreciation	$ 62,500	
	Cost of money	150,000	
	Acid needs one fourth of 12,922 tons,		
	3,230 tons at $73.50	237,405	
	Sludge conversion:		
	12,922 × 1.5 = 19,383 × $23.70*	459,377	
	Total		$909,282
1983	Depreciation	$ 62,500	
	Cost of money	150,000	
	Acid needs one fourth of 13,245 tons,		
	3,311 tons at $78.50	259,913	
	Sludge conversion:		
	13,245 × 1.5 = 19,867 × $23.55*	467,867	
	Total		$940,280

Assumptions:
Acid cost will continue to increase at rate of $5 per year.
Consumption will increase at rate of 2½ percent per year.
*Cost per ton decreases as capacity utilization increases.

224

EXHIBIT Iv

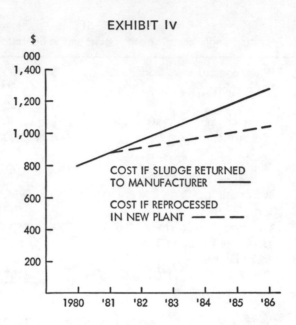

EXHIBIT V

At present company uses 12,000 tons of acid a year. One half of the sludge treated can be converted into usable acid. Reconverted acid equals 75 percent of original acid used. Thus:

50 percent sludge = 75 percent of 12,000 tons
Sludge = 2 (3/4 × 12,000) = 18,000 tons

Plant capacity: 100 tons P/Day × 365 days = 36,500 tons P/A. So, conversion plant will operate at 50 percent capacity. Since 12,000 tons of acid produces 18,000 tons of sludge and this converts back to 9,000 tons of acid, it takes 2 tons of sludge to make 1 ton of acid. At 50 percent capacity it costs $24 to treat one ton of sludge so reconverted acid will cost $48 a ton. As capacity utilization increases cost will drop until 100 percent capacity is reached at which point reconverted acid will cost $32 a ton.

EXHIBIT VI

Year	Projected costs if sludge is returned to manufacturer		Projected costs if reconversion plant is built	
1981	$ 878,954		$ 879,415	
1982	965,527		909,282	
1983	1,055,887	$2,900,368	940,280	$2,727,977
1984	$1,120,000		$ 980,000	
1985	1,200,000		1,010,000	
1986	1,280,000	3,600,000	1,040,000	3,030,000
		$6,500,368		$5,757,977

Analysis of Callaghan's report

You will note that while the decision is the final entry on the outline, it appears first in the report because Callaghan wanted Marlow to be aware of his recommendation as soon as he started to read. Patrick had made his decision, and whether it was right or wrong, he had no intention of trying to hide it near the end of the text.

Callaghan delivered the report to Marlow's secretary on the appointed day and returned to his office. To his surprise the palms of his hands were a trifle damp, and the breakfast he had recently eaten lay in a solid lump somewhere between his gullet and his stomach.

Marlow read the report quickly, spent ten minutes considering the exhibits, and then reread the text at a much slower pace. When he was done, he grunted once, picked up his pen, wrote at the top of the first page, "I agree," and signed his name with a flourish. He called his secretary, handed her the report and said, "Give copies of this to all members of the Executive Committee immediately and put it on the agenda for tomorrow's meeting."

He called after her as she was leaving his office. "Tell Callaghan he did a good job."

Why was Marlow pleased with the report? He must have had his reasons. I'm going to make a list of the factors that might have influenced Marlow to approve Callaghan's recommendation.

1. Patrick did exactly what he was asked to do. He followed his assignment and held the text to 800 words.
2. He opened with his recommendation. Marlow knew where he was going from the start and was able to relate every statement in the report to the recommendation. He found no inconsistencies in the argument.
3. The headings made for easy reading.
4. Following the outline ensured that the report was cohesive, flowed smoothly without sudden changes in direction.
5. The report was honest. Patrick didn't choose a course of action and ignore other alternatives. He identified the disadvantages as well as the advantages of each alternative, and when he made his choice, he supported it with hard evidence.
6. He made a clear distinction between facts and assumptions and demonstrated to the best of his ability the reasonableness of the assumptions he was forced to make.
7. The exhibits were clear and well constructed. Marlow could have looked at them before he read the report and understood them perfectly. They were self-sufficient, well labeled.
8. The text did not waste time in explaining how the exhibits were prepared.
9. The writing was simple, clear, and strong. True, for the

most part sentences were short, but perhaps the terse, no-nonsense style added an element of persuasiveness to the writing.

10. Callaghan made his recommendation with full confidence in its validity. He didn't waffle, leave himself safety hatches to escape through.

11. His judgment was good, his reasoning sound. Marlow found no flaws in his analysis. There was no reason for Marlow not to go along with Patrick's conclusions.

All these points refer to mechanical or attitudinal elements in the report. There is another aspect we should also consider. The Gold Nugget problem involves both knowns and unknowns. Among the knowns are: ecological regulations, exhaustion of capacity to dispose of sludge, accelerated price rise in acid cost during previous two years. These issues have to do with the past or the present. When we probe the future, we enter the realm of the unknown. Will inflation be with us for the next decade? At what rate will it continue? Where will acid prices be next year, five years from now? Will construction costs advance at 10 percent a year or double within five years? What are the possibilities that instead of rising, prices will fall?

There may have been a time when the economy remained stable over an extended period. How much more simple must have been the art of management in such an utopian era. It does not seem likely that we will soon see a return to such a favorable environment. Thus, the art of management more and more involves the ability to judge the trends of the future. To do this, the manager must be thoroughly familiar with the present situation of his organization, and in addition he must keep current with the influences affecting his industry. Most importantly he must base his plans not only on where his company is now, but where he expects it to be in five or ten years or even further in the future. This planning involves an increasing number of variables, which become more complex daily.

An evaluation of variables must be based on a sound analysis of the basic forces at work on the economy, but all the analysis in the world will not guarantee a correct answer. There comes a time when a manager is forced to rely on intuitive judgment. A statistical approach is fine—it deals with probabilities. Years ago I was involved for a time in developing a rather complex gearing system. Three individual gears were included in the train. The first and second had an efficiency quotient of 90 percent, the third 70 percent. Mathematics told us the energy output would be 56.7 percent of the input, but what chance would we have had of designing an adequate system if we could only guess at the efficiency of each part of the system?

So it is with the statistical approach. If we apply probabilities to each segment of our equation, our answer can only be as accurate as our applied probabilities. This is where intuitive judgment comes in.

Patrick Callaghan was not afraid to rely on his intuition after he had analyzed to the best of his ability, using all the information at his disposal. Then, although realizing the course of action he proposed involved a risk that he might be wrong, he came out with his recommendation in no uncertain terms. That took guts, and Patrick has the stuff of which top-grade managers are made.

12

Conclusion

I don't quite know how to wrap up this half of the book or how to write a gracious close for the whole work. Perhaps I have shot my entire wad and have nothing left to say.

Assuming this to be the actual case, all that remains for me to do is to thank you for having read this far and to hope what I have had to say has been helpful to you.

Nice to have known you. Good luck.

W. G. Ryckman